Creative Procedures
for Adult Groups

HAROLD D. MINOR, editor

Creative Procedures
for Adult Groups

ABINGDON PRESS
Nashville New York

CREATIVE PROCEDURES FOR ADULT GROUPS

Copyright © 1966, 1967, 1968 by Abingdon Press

ISBN 0-687-09833-5

Library of Congress Catalog Card Number: 68-27624

Scripture quotations unless otherwise noted are
from the Revised Standard Version of the Bible,
copyrighted 1946 and 1952 by the Division of
Christian Education, National Council of Churches
and are used by permission.

Scripture quotation noted Phillips is from *The New
Testament in Modern English,* copyright 1958 by
J. B. Phillips.

SET UP, PRINTED, AND BOUND BY THE
PARTHENON PRESS, AT NASHVILLE,
TENNESSEE, UNITED STATES OF AMERICA

To *Mary* *Ruth* *and*
our *three* *sons*
Mike, *Sterling,* *and* *Gary*

Contents

CONTENTS

Introduction

An adult educator wrote to me, "We need a book to help teachers and leadership teams learn how to lead groups. We especially need guidance on specific teaching procedures, showing how to use each procedure in particular areas of study."

This book is a response to that letter. All the interpretations of procedures contained here in edited form appeared first in *Adult Teacher*. I am indebted to the writers for their kind permission to use their original manuscripts in more or less modified form; also, I want to express grateful appreciation to Maxine Stout, who edited the original copy.

Behind the selection of the procedures that appear here lie certain assumptions about adult education. These appeared in a previous book, *New Ways for a New Day:*

1. The primary setting for Christian learning is the community of faith.
2. Learning occurs when a person sees the meaning of

an idea or experience for his own condition and changes according to this meaning.

3. Learning results from personal involvement more than through a process of "pouring into an empty cup."

4. Previous experience and present situation affect a person's will to learn; so knowledge of the learner helps a leader plan more effectively.

5. Christian education of adults is related to all aspects of life, including but not limited to the Bible.

6. Adults should be involved in many approaches to learning, in respect to both content and procedures.

7. Adults should help to set goals for their own learning and help to decide how to reach these goals.

8. Leadership is exercised both by *being* a person who influences learning and by *functioning* in leadership roles.

9. Genuine *Christian* education of adults will result in capable participants in the church's fellowship and in its mission in the world.

In our culture we are bombarded by news from all the world. From newspapers and magazines, T.V. and radio, we learn about space and medicine, about our bodies and our spirits, about literature and art, about improving our marriage and raising children, about political problems, social and economic problems, and international relations. One of the challenges to all ministers in this day, and to all laymen as ministers, is to know something about many aspects of the whole culture.

This total culture creates many kinds of intersections.

An intersection is a "model" of how persistent human concerns meet the gospel. Intersection is also a model of where Christian education takes place, but another model is necessary for us to think about what goes on there. At the intersection what happens is *interaction* among persons. This interaction is important because no one who teaches a class or study group can know all that needs to be known. And certainly no one person can be aware of all the problems and questions that people bring to the situation.

When we confront one another at the intersection, we can offer not only information, but insights, feelings, and attitudes as well. The role of the teacher or leader needs to be almost the reverse today of what it has been in the past. The teacher ought to be asking questions, not just to see if people know factual answers, but to stimulate thought—to help persons move from one stage of inquiry to the next higher stage. Sometimes, of course, one must give information, but a much more important task of the teacher or the leadership team is to formulate questions that will cause people to think through problems (including securing the information they need).

We have tried to give some stimulus to this process in this book. The basic position is that every person who is involved in study should have an opportunity to see how he might deal with the study material in two or three alternative ways. The leadership team or teacher should be relieved from the responsibility of answering informational questions as much as possible. Instead, procedures should be used that will stimulate thought based on the experiences and backgrounds of all the persons who are involved. The procedures treated here are intended to aid such involvement.

Motives for learning: In *Toward a Theory of Instruction,* in a chapter entitled "The Will to Learn," Jerome Bruner suggests four motives for learning that are essential in the education of adults. These are intrinsic motives, based on satisfaction in the actual learning experience, not on external rewards. They are essential because most adults in educational situations are present voluntarily.

First, says Bruner, is the motive of *curiosity.* Adults have an innate desire to know, to learn, to settle the problems that confront them. This curiosity can best be stimulated by a presentation that creates uncertainty; for example, if we do the unexpected, if we leave a gap in their thinking, if we set up a situation in which they may try to control their own learning. Adults need to learn to learn under their own self-direction. That is, when I have the opportunity to decide what I want to learn and then I base my study on the interests I express, I have a built-in reason for learning.

Bruner next mentions the drive toward *competence.* Most adults desire to be able. But to gain a sense of accomplishment we need a plan for learning: a beginning, a feeling of going somewhere, and an ending. We gain confidence as we begin, continue, and see the end of a particular study. We must also be able in some way to measure progress in the kind of competence toward which we are striving. Finally, we must do some stretching and gain some sense of going beyond what we already know, if we are to say we are growing in competence.

A third motive, says Bruner, is that of *identification.*
We have competence models, persons we look to as being
competent. This is a very important point for Bruner, that
the teacher or the leader of a group serve as a competence
model for the members of his group. He does this, *not*
by saying, "This is what I do—do it like this," but by en-
gaging each of the students in a roundtable dialogue, asking the kinds of questions that open the student up to
himself. That is, the teacher becomes a part of the student's
internal dialogue. He serves not as one who provides the
answers for the student, but as one who reveals to each
student new possibilities within himself.

Reciprocity is the fourth motive that Bruner points out.
For illustration he reminds us of the experience of getting
a car stuck in the mud or snow. Five or six persons come
and put their shoulders to the body as they rock the car
forward and backward. There is no plan—no one has
drawn a diagram, no one has taught them how—but somehow they all know that they must rock together. Reciprocity is fitting into such a total enterprise, just leaning
oneself into it whenever appropriate. This is something
that is not so much told, as felt. There is, Bruner says,
in every one of us a built-in need, a desire, and a capability
for this kind of working together, this fitting into an
operation.

I have been amazed, as you may have been, at many people who have said, "We can't discuss, we can't talk, we
don't know enough. You tell us the answers, you are the
teacher, you know the truth." When persons who have said
this have gotten into an intersection where the expectation was that they would share of their own lives, they've

done it. The leader's task is to create such an intersection with such interaction. Every procedure in this book is intended to help you do just this.

Increasing our creativity: How we neglect the creative potential that is found in every person! We're very likely to pay attention to those who have high I.Q.'s and to ignore those who can make new things out of old things. One of the reasons we do this, I suppose, is that we have been trained in convergent thinking—in looking for the right answers. Now, we need convergent thinking, we need to work toward solutions, certainly—but we need to go in every direction to find these answers. To do this, we need to encourage divergent, open-ended thinking.

Creativity is not all of the same kind. In George F. Kneller's *The Art and Science of Creativity,* a paragraph written by Harry Broudy has to do with the range of creativity:

"Invention, scientific thinking and esthetic creation do have in common a facility for the rearranging of previously experienced elements into new configurations. When Sandburg says that 'the fog creeps in on little cat feet' and a child calls eraser scraps 'mistake dust' and the painter shows the four sides of a barn at once (cubism) and a writer speaks of something as being 'as relentless as a taxi meter' and a man converts a sled runner into a wheel and Newton sees the analogy between apples and planets, there is manifest an activity of mind that seems to be of the same weave, despite the difference of coloration." [1]

[1] (New York: Holt, Rinehart & Winston, 1965), p. 12.

The meaning of this paragraph for us may be that there are varieties of gifts, but one ministry; a variety of members, but one body. The problem is, we may confine our attention to the one gift of thinking and the one member of the body, the brain, to the neglect of other members of the body and other kinds of gifts, especially the gift of creativity. Everyone has some kind of creative potential. Our job as teachers is to release this potential that is in every person—it's part of God's gift to each one, but it's stifled by the whole educational system. Some of the obstacles to our use of this creativity are: habit, convention, fear, the desire for reward and success, the quest for certainty, and the inability to play.

How does creativity work? Consider a kaleidoscope. You turn it around, back and forth, and the little bits and pieces of material in the front end form different patterns. This is a kind of model of the way creativity works within us. The more bits and pieces of information we have, the more likely we are to come up with combinations that will mean something.

The creative problem-solving process is one way of trying to foster creativity in others. To solve a given problem (for example, one that might arise in a study unit on the mission of the church), the first thing to do is to *find out all the facts* we possibly can about it. We may ask such questions as these: What do I need to know? Where shall I find this information? What is this situation really like? What am I trying to accomplish?

After we ask these questions and find the facts, we *restate the problem*. We try to put into two words, a noun and a verb, what we're trying to accomplish. If we see clearly what we're working for, then the problem becomes how to accomplish it.

Our next step is *idea finding*. A necessary reminder to ourselves when we're trying to get our minds in gear, is to suspend judgment. To get many ideas we use brainstorming (see page 46). The only way to get a lot of ideas flowing from many people is to overcome our tendency to judge, to discuss, or to evaluate when a person puts an idea out. But how do we get the *most* ideas in brainstorming?

There are certain idea-spurring questions that we can ask ourselves or others in the group. For instance, How can we *adapt* what we already are doing or what we already have? Another question is, What can we *alter?* How can we make it larger or smaller? Another is, What could we *substitute* for something that is going on now? Or, How could we *rearrange* what is now happening or what we have talked about? Could we reverse the order? And then, How can we *combine* these various suggestions?

After we've gotten all these ideas out there comes the stage of *incubation*. Don't try to decide immediately; let the ideas percolate. If we're really thinking and praying hard, illumination may come.

The next stage involves *evaluation and decision*. Some of the criteria to use as you decide on a solution are these: Is it simple? Is it true to human nature? Can I write out a clear statement? Does my idea explode in people's minds? Is this the right time? Could someone else present it better? What if the whole proposal were just the opposite from what we're suggesting? What are we leaving out?

We evaluate solutions, using such criteria, and choose

the one that appears best. Then we have to decide how to *get our solution implemented.* Here we ask: In what ways might we gain acceptance? How might we dramatize it? How might we anticipate objections? Who can we get to help us? Where shall this be done? Also, When is the best time for doing this? Finally, What precautions should we take as we try something new? Creative problem solving is a kind of circular process. When one problem reaches solution we simply have a new problem, that of implementation.

One purpose of each procedure found here is to unleash the creative potential in each individual. But remember —nothing threatens the established situation like helping people to be their true and full selves, to express their ideas honestly. That's revolutionary, as the gospel always has been.

Overview: A Look at the Learning Process

As You Plan for Teaching/Learning

As you plan, consider six aspects of group study. The aspects, indicated by verbs, are: *sensitize, organize, research, share, decide,* and *act.*

Sensitize: How can you help your class recognize the issues dealt with in a unit of study? What can you as a teacher do to sensitize your class members to the reality and importance of the issue? How can the issues (topics) to be studied become concrete, human, and significant for your class members? What knowledge of, or experience with, the basic content in this unit does your class already have?

What questions do you ask yourself as you begin to

plan? Perhaps these: What are the basic issues, and how can I help the class see that these issues are not trumped-up but are real issues affecting the class members? What can I do to help my class members recognize their reality and importance? Early in your planning you must answer these questions for yourself as leader.

Suppose, for example, the subject of the study is "Art as Response to God's Love." You may choose to brainstorm and discuss this question: What are some ways our local church is already related to art, art forms, and aesthetics? (Consider hymnals, organs, choirs, architecture, symbols, stained glass, and so forth.) Your class will see that the relationship between the church and the arts is inescapable. Then questions about the quality and character of that relationship can be asked.

In general, whatever the topic being studied, the leader needs to *sensitize* the class to the issue.

Organize: Adults are going to retain very little they do not learn for themselves; they are going to learn very little they do not *discover* for themselves. *Organize your class for discovery.* A teacher organizes a class when he selects a teaching method or class procedure. Panel discussions organize the class in one way; field trips, in another. Hundreds of teaching methods are available to you.[1] Select methods that cause the adult to *discover* for himself (individually or through group action) what he will attempt to learn.

[1] See the list appended to *The Group Workshop Way in the Local Church,* by Paul Douglass (New York: Association Press, 1956).

For example, if your class is considering the question, How does (or should) the church work with the architect as artist? two possible procedures are (1) read about the problem, (2) interview architects who have worked with churches frequently. Of these, the second will probably yield the more durable learning because it requires the initiative of the learner and diminishes passivity. The second procedure requires the class to (1) *discover* architects with an interest in the church, (2) *enlist* their aid, (3) *formulate* for them a clear statement of the issue, (4) *plan* for the interview by selecting key questions and a guiding purpose, (5) *digest* the interview by reviewing and evaluating it afterward. Initiative, exploration, and active, self-directed discovery mark each of these five steps. Organize your class for discovery. Select methods and procedures accordingly.

Research: Research is a rather academic name for *disciplined seeking.* Serious study requires research, a persistent seeking after new facts, new values, and new experiences. What kind of disciplines can make possible the seeking that adult education in the church requires? *Reading* is one such discipline.

Most adults think they can read, but most adults in the church school do not read—at least with reference to church school. Teachers are responsible for guiding students in disciplined seeking, which suggests that teachers are responsible for their students' reading habits and skills. Some church school classes need to study *How to Read a Book,* by Mortimer J. Adler. Other classes need to study, as a group, their own reading habits. How much time do members spend reading? What do they read? What books? What magazines? What motivates their reading? What attitudes do they have toward reading books and periodicals recommended by the church school? What affects the amount of time they spend reading in preparation for church school? Reading is of little value to a student who cannot clarify and organize his own thoughts. *The Art of Clear Thinking* by Rudolf Flesch can help your class achieve new skills in the organization and clarification of ideas.

Research, even when disciplined by strong reading and thinking skills, needs to be directed toward *resources*. The teacher does not do research *for* the class, but he puts the class on the trail by directing it toward basic sources of information. A teacher of adults in the church school needs, at the very least, a close knowledge of several English translations of the Bible, the best study editions of the Bible, several one-volume and multivolume commentaries on the Bible, and a good Bible dictionary.

In your teaching assume that the entire class is responsible for the disciplined seeking of new facts, new values, and new experiences.

Share: *Sensitize, organize, research,* the first three steps, are followed by the fourth, *share*. Sharing is essential to Christian community; sharing, then, is essential to your church school class. Some facts can be learned by the isolated individual, but values can be learned best with other people. A church is a group of people committed to sharing their faith, values, and worship. A church school class can make that sharing informed, disciplined, and deliberate.

What is shared in a church school class? Fundamentally, personalities. New values, new experiences, and new perspectives are essentially *personal* realities. If the gospel brings "newness," and if the class is growing in its grasp of the gospel, then new life and new values will be shared. The sharing that goes on in the church school should be *informed* by group research, *disciplined* by reading and thinking skills that have been deliberately sharpened, and *consciously selected* by the class.

The sharing that Christian education requires is neither casual nor superficial. Rather, it is a sharing that goes to the roots of personal growth: a sharing of faith *and* doubt, insight *and* ignorance, triumphs *and* failures, hopes *and* fears. Christian growth occurs through the mutual enrichment of Christian personalities by one another.

A teacher will examine his conduct of a class to see if it makes possible such sharing. Certainly the typical class is miles from such personal interaction. Few classes recognize such sharing as a legitimate, let alone necessary, means of Christian education. A responsible class will study and evaluate its own group life in order to find ways to foster sharing. Your class may begin by studying *Members One of Another,* a 59-frame color filmstrip with script and guide, available from your denominational bookstore.

Sharing depends upon two things: (1) basic trust within the group and (2) communications skills. How can communication become more precise? How can barriers to communication be identified, and how do they arise? How do nonverbal forms of communication color what we

24

intend to say with words? Such questions as these and others can be studied in the film *More Than Words* (16mm, 20 minutes; available from your denominational bookstore).

Decide and act: What decisions and actions result from study in your church school class? Your teaching is ineffective unless the students follow through their learning to decision and action. Learning is a form of growth and change. When growth and change are not observable in the decisions and actions that follow study, the validity of the learning is doubtful. A study of the gospel is a study of those realities (God, Christ, redemption, and love, for example) that affect us most centrally. To suppose, then, that we can study the gospel without undergoing growth and change is to suppose that the gospel affects us only at the margins of our lives. Expect change in the students because they have studied the gospel together. This is basic.

The teacher should plan every unit of study in the light of these questions: How can the insights of this unit affect the way the students make decisions? What actions do these insights suggest? What particular decisions do my students face that can be either empowered or illumined by this study?

At times your class should deliberately plan a course of action that will show that they have learned. Such action will reinforce what has been learned and enhance the possibility that it will last. Field trips, service projects, further study, community action, new responsibilities within the church itself—these are a few examples of actions that may reinforce and express group study.

As group study renews your power to decide and act on behalf of the gospel, your class should regularly ask, What is the connection between our study as a class and our actions on behalf of the gospel? Unless a class (or teacher) plans for the consideration of this question in relation to every unit of study, it may be ignored because of the pain and guilt caused by facing it.

Learning theory and Christian ethics support one another in an interesting way at this point. Learning theory suggests that until we "act out" what we learn, we do not learn it securely. Actions based on newly learned facts and attitudes bolster and nail down those facts and attitudes. In a similar way Christian ethics suggests that our obedience to the will of God verifies our hearing his will. Until we obey, who can say we have heard his will? *Decide and act* is sound counsel, pedagogically and ethically.

A teacher who plans his work with reference to these verbs—*sensitize, organize, research, share, decide,* and *act* —will probably plan well.

How Do Ideas Get into a Class?

New ideas are the raw material of learning. Yet adult classes often resist new ideas. Class discussions, then, become poverty-stricken, with worn-out thoughts rehashed session after session. New ideas may be kept out of a class by conditions like these.

1. Laziness, apathy, and a lack of initiative
2. A feeling that anything new in religion is to be regarded with suspicion
3. An authoritarian teacher
4. An authoritarian class procedure
5. An unwillingness to risk change
6. An ignorance of resources
7. A lack of research skill
8. An ignorance of techniques for getting ideas into the class
9. Inadequate planning

Here are some suggestions that will help your class overcome some common barriers to new ideas.

Present new ideas unselfconsciously and with confidence. A new idea may fail to be heard if it is presented with so little confidence that it emerges trembling, covered with apologies. Confidence in presenting a new idea is not the same as arrogance in holding an idea. To present a new idea apologetically draws attention to the person who feels a need to apologize, rather than to the idea itself. A person presenting an idea apologetically is a person sending out distress signals. The sympathetic listener is far more likely to hear the distress signals than the new idea.

Relate new ideas to the total discussion. Each session should have stated goals, a suggested direction, and a few key ideas that give the whole session an identifiable framework. Each new idea offered during the session, whether offered by the teacher or a class member, needs to be related as it is presented to the total session. When the teacher or a class member introduces an idea that does not clearly contribute to the stated goals and framework of the session, the class may see little reason to bother with that idea. A class can receive and use new ideas when those ideas fall into a meaningful setting.

A meaningful setting for a given session is best established by an overview of the whole session, stated by the teacher early in the session and shared by the class throughout the session. The ideas we already have are docking points for new ideas. A class learning together as a group needs a cluster of docking points that are shared, largely, by the whole class. As new ideas enter the thoughts of the class, they can be received if they are deliberately related to the ideas already shared and accepted by the group as a framework for that session.

Pace the presentation of new ideas with care. A new idea may fail to be heard if it is presented too rapidly for assimilation. New ideas in religion cannot be assimilated as fast as new ideas in less personal areas. The teacher must pace his presentation of new ideas according to the class's ability to digest new ideas. *Generally, the more threatening an idea is, the more slowly it will be understood.* Also, the more abstract an idea is, the more slowly it will be understood.

Threatening ideas are ideas that challenge seriously what a person thinks or does. A sensitive teacher will recognize threatening ideas in advance; he will plan his teaching so as to reduce the degree of threat as much as possible *without cutting the heart out of the idea.* Until a class hears, understands, evaluates, and applies a new idea, there is little wisdom in moving to still newer ideas.

If you express an idea that I have already accepted, I can hear you easily and accurately. What you say does not threaten me. I can listen to you and retain the same values I have already embraced. If you say something that confirms and undergirds what I already believe, I can easily remember what you have said. A good teacher needs to recall frequently the principle stated by Goodwin Watson: "People remember new information which confirms their previous attitudes better than they remember new information which runs counter to their previous attitudes." New ideas, then, have an intrinsic disadvantage as compared to familiar ideas, since *new ideas almost always call for some form of personal readjustment.* Values and beliefs may have to change if new ideas are heard. A teacher, then, needs to present new ideas compassionately, knowing that they cannot be learned without struggle and pain.

New ideas get inside a class effectively only if they get in at the right time. For example, a class is not ready to understand the meaning of Israel's infidelity as interpreted by Hosea until it first understands the meaning of the covenant as described in Exodus.

A teacher is sometimes impressed with his ability to present many new ideas to a class in rapid sequence. But a sensitive teacher, unconcerned about impressing the class but very much concerned about the class's assimilation of each new idea, will pace his presentation. He will give continuing thought to both the sequence and the speed with which he presents new ideas. He will, through free discussion, be constantly testing the readiness of the class to move on. His personal agenda will not overshadow the pace set by the class itself.

Teach so that new ideas enter the class from many sources. New ideas may fail to be heard if they always originate with the teacher or with any other one person. A teacher may feel obligated by his office to feed new ideas into the class. He is, as it were, duty bound to take the initiative. But initiative that is not shared can be tyrannical, even when benevolent. Tyranny may induce either apathy or rebellion in the class. A teacher who is the sole source of new ideas within a class may be a dedicated tyrant. Apathetic classes are usually the result, because class members usually feel less guilt over apathy than they would over outright rebellion. However, apathy itself is a way of rejecting the teacher and his ideas. So, if only the teacher or any other one person brings new ideas to the class, an apathetic rejection of these ideas is likely.

A class needs many centers of initiative. The good teacher is the one who fosters initiative by all the class members so that ideas enter it from every quarter. He will control his own initiative. He will say and share perhaps less than he knows, so that class members will be forced to discover for themselves some ideas that he would otherwise be giving them, pablum-style. When every member feels that he is part of the show, he is more likely to take in the whole show.

Be aware of how the congeniality of a group affects its readiness to face new ideas. A congenial atmosphere, touched with easy humor and goodwill, is almost essential to the facing of new ideas. A group of strangers, even if they bear some name such as "the Young Couples Class," is poor soil for learning. When I am with a stranger—even though we have been acquainted for years—I am preoccupied with our mutual strangeness. I am hardly ready to learn with him about deeply personal matters, such as faith, love, and obedience. A good teacher will be just as conscious of the climate within a class as with the lesson material he brings to the class.

Congeniality can grow within a class only when the members have the time, the freedom, and the will to interact with one another. The teacher who dominates his class is frustrating the interaction of the members one with another. He is obstructing the growth of trust, familiarity, and goodwill among the members. He is therefore defeating his own teaching. The use of only such teaching methods as lecturing, in ways that allow the students to interact only with the teacher and the subject matter, blocks the growth of congeniality within the group and thus hampers learning itself.

A new idea may fail to be heard if the student feels he is unimportant to the life of the class. "To put it bluntly, Teacher, if you don't care about me, I don't care about your new ideas." Such an attitude may sound vengeful when stated that boldly, but the principle is firmly established that the student who does not feel wanted is not likely to learn much. There is no need to interpret this principle sentimentally, because we can measure rather objectively the degree to which a student is wanted in a group.

The student is wanted to the degree that he is allowed and encouraged to participate. If you draw a circle around the members of a class who participate, you have drawn a circle around the effective life and membership of the class. You have also drawn a circle around the members who feel that they are wanted and that their continued presence matters to the others. You have also drawn a circle around those members who are learning and growing.

Finally, clarify each new idea by contrasting it with opposing ideas. The learning of a new idea is facilitated by a skillful use of *contrast*. An idea is not clear until it has been distinguished from its contraries. For example, the Christian idea that pride is sin cannot be understood until pride is contrasted with legitimate self-esteem. Or again, democracy cannot be understood until it is contrasted with totalitarianism. Students often reject a new idea before it is clarified; they reject it because of their misunderstanding of it.

The skillful presentation of a new idea, therefore, must include clarification by contrast. Until a class understands an idea well enough to contrast it with contrary ideas, they do not understand it well enough to accept it or reject it. Until a teacher understands an idea well enough to make significant contrasts he does not understand it well enough to present it fairly. Anyone, therefore, who wishes to present a new idea to a class should examine his proposed presentation to see if the idea is precisely formulated and clarified through the skillful use of contrast.

Using Personal Creativity

Creative problem-solving, as outlined in the Introduction, is not the only way to release the creative potential in adults. The procedures in this section are especially useful in drawing forth personal expressions and pushing back persons' horizons of awareness.

One form of human learning is by *self-investment.* As learners, we combine (1) our cognition, or knowledge and way of thinking, (2) our identity, or understanding of who we are, and (3) our self-esteem, or level of opinion about ourselves, into an estimate of our competence or sufficiency as a person. Then under our own self-control, with some new creative twist, with full intensity of commitment, and with truth about us exposed, we invest this self-competence in the situation that confronts us.

This investment of self is mainly a letting go, to the extent of risking anguish, as we attempt to bridge the distance between ourselves and another person. In this attempt we seek for a sign from the other person confirming us as being accepted. If we receive a positive signal of acceptance, our sense of worth is confirmed, and it is likely that whatever enhances the other person then will enhance our own sense of worth. If we are rejected, of course, the tendency is toward conflict and cross purposes. And the heart of the investment of ourselves is this risk of the anguish of rejection and conflict. But if confirmed, we incorporate the positive response into our new and enhanced mental image of our self-competence, based on a new synthesis of cognition, identity, and self-esteem.

We are all somewhat like the woman who said, "I don't know what I think until I hear myself say it!" We can learn what we think and feel, not only by saying it, but by acting it out, by putting another's words into our own, by saying the first thing that comes to mind, by recalling forgotten images and feelings, or by moving in unaccustomed ways. These procedures, in short, can lead us to new self-understanding, as well as to new ideas and ways of acting.

Using Experiences from Life

One of the marks of vital classroom discussion is that it strikes the life experience of the participants. They are emotionally involved in the class operation because part of them is at stake in it. There is aliveness, and each person knows it. Insight occurs. New ideas are formulated. There is struggle. There is breakthrough. People get the feeling that something real is happening. And it is. Once one tastes this type of educational transaction, everything else is flat.

How does it happen?

Anyone who thinks he has *the* answer is simple-minded. Sometimes it happens on its own without planning. Sometimes it does not happen in spite of planning. But usually when a creative educational moment occurs, it is because what is said or thought or done is related to life as it is among those involved. This provides a guideline: In classroom procedure look for ways to relate the ideas being studied to the real life experience of class members. One way to do this is to use as raw material the experiences of the class members. For instance, if Christian vocations are being studied, get examples from the workaday world of the class members to form the *basis* for the study of the various aspects of the problem.

Real experience brings relevance: A person who knows how and has the freedom to put into a discussion an experience from his own life helps the groups in several ways.

First, he guarantees his own interest. Anyone who will commit part of his personal experience will follow the discussion with complete interest. His interest is often contagious and has the potential of arousing the interest of the whole class.

Second, participants know the experience is real because it comes from a real person. A general case history always has an air of make-believe around it. Class members say, "This never happened to me." But when a class member comes up with a concrete experience, the realness is evident.

Third, an example from the experience of a class member allows for checking. In an anonymous case study, there is no way of filling in an obscure detail. On the other hand, if a question is raised about an experience of a class member, the detail can be verified. This often means the difference between discovering a new idea or not. Consider the following example:

"Do you really mean, Sam, that your boss stuck out his neck on hiring a handicapped person when management advised him against it?"

"That's it exactly. Because he believes in the worth of the human being, he was willing to take risks."

"I don't believe it."

"Okay. I invite you to lunch next week with me and the boss. We'll talk about it, and you can make up your own mind."

The lunch was set up, and the doubter was impressed. This could be done only because the class was dealing with a live experience.

How to find experience from life: The crucial question in the use of live material is, Where do you get it? Many persons are reluctant to put their own experiences into the hopper for discussion or study. They may think them not very important. Shyness prevents others from ever venturing their own experiences. The time that it takes to organize one's presentation might be another deterrent. These and other obstacles will not stop a creative class from making use of their own experiences as raw material for discussion if they are persistent.

For instance, one way to get at the material in the lives of a group is to get a problem defined. Take, for example, the problem of honesty in merchandising. Formulate a question: In your daily work how do you experience this problem? In a freely talkative group examples might pop immediately. These examples can be listed and grouped, and further questions formulated for more study. But if the group is slow to contribute, how can you help them present this vital material?

One way would be to formulate the problem and the question, as shown above. Then ask the group members to pair off and talk about it for ten minutes. Ask each pair to make a list of examples. This list is a big help for the shy person making a report.

Or the group members may be invited to list their examples on a sheet of paper; then in pairs each person tells the other of his experiences. Finally, these examples can be reported to the group. Unusual examples might be selected for special study. One or more examples could lead to a real action project. Let us say that it was discovered that a certain merchant in town was selling irregular sweaters at premium prices. What action could be taken by the class members to protect the public?

Thus, the dimension of action—which is the ultimate in every educational enterprise—is added to a study of how the problems are caused and to the Christian understanding of the problem.

Once a class gets experience in using examples from their own lives, they will be able to do it with more skill, and the whole level of the learning activity will be upgraded.

Recalling Childhood Experiences

Playing make-believe is a natural part of every child's experience. We like to pretend to be what we think we have the potential for being. We like to dream of involvement in other events. We enjoy playing roles. Sometimes the play experiences closely parallel our actual experiences; other times they do not. But always such role playing is very real to us at the time.

An insight into childhood experiences can be a useful learning technique for us as adults. Childhood is the time when we test values and relationships and select by trial and error those experiences that apply and have meaning for our view of life.

Reliving events of earlier years can be most enjoyable. Think of the people who influenced your life most. Make a list of the ten most memorable people in your childhood and what you remember about them. Were they people who helped you learn how to treat other people? Were they the friends who led you patiently through new experiences in which you gained new knowledge? Or were they persons whose conduct left a negative impression? Then think of some event that is typical of your relationships with one of these people. Was it in school, home, church, or community? Did the situation make a contribution to your learning experiences as a child? How did other people present interact with you and the key person in the episode?

Finally, ask yourself two questions about what you think was learned.

First, what were your immediate conclusions *at the time?* That is, as a child what did you think you learned? Was it a satisfying experience or not? Do you remember repeating the same type of experience again, seeking further relationship or understanding, or by accident did the same experience teach something new? What happened the next time?

Second, as you view your childhood experience, do you detect any signs that you were learning something more or different or helpful of which you were not aware at the time? If so, how was such learning used and applied in your later childhood and maturity?

By such self-understanding we can gain useful insights and understanding into how we see the world and the people in it. More important, we can see how we learn as individuals and how we learn in relation to other people and events. Recalling childhood experiences is an exercise in revealing how we learned our values, hopes, prejudices, desires, and dislikes. Usually we can summarize such learning in one or more of four areas, although many experiences cannot be easily categorized.

First, we learn to understand how and why we do or do not trust ourselves and others. This is an important understanding for all growing people. We can use our capacities to their fullest only if we trust them and trust people enough to venture forth into new and unknown experiences.

Second, we learn to share what we are and what we have. Everyone has something unique to contribute: his own individuality. This is our Christian faith, and this is our experience when we are open to all persons. In childhood we sometimes have experiences that tend to make us question this basic fact of life. Persons whose own lives are warped and limited sometimes tend to curb children's probing and learning because they cannot tolerate seeing children having experiences that contradict their own twisted view of life. In recalling such experiences we can learn how we developed our view of ourselves and our ability to contribute to others. We can see whether we may have underestimated our unique value as a person and as God's unique creation in his world.

Third, we can learn to appreciate other people as unique individuals created by God with potential for growth and with their own contributions to make in God's continuing plan of creation. Helping others to grow helps us grow. If we look carefully at our childhood experiences, we may find that the most influential persons in our lives have been those who appreciated us as individuals and provided us the opportunity to be ourselves, to learn from our experiences, and to be growing persons.

Fourth, we can learn how we fit into the world, into God's plan of creation, into the lives of others who want and need us. One of the most helpful childhood experiences we ever have is to discover how much we are needed by someone else. It may have been a playmate, a companion walking to school, a confidant in time of joy or sorrow, or a colleague in getting homework finished. Someone needed us; we needed someone else for life to be complete. Recognizing this now will help us be more secure in our relationships with everyone. We are not needed in exactly the same way by every person we encounter, but we are needed.

Childhood is a prime time of learning. By examining the experiences of our childhood we can learn much that will help us continue our growth, expand our use of our talents, and enrich our relationships with others. We may also learn to help others develop themselves in these same ways.

Role Playing

"Let him who is without sin among you be the first to throw a stone at her" (John 8:7). In these words Jesus was giving instructions for a kind of role playing. The excited people who brought to him the woman caught in adultery were no longer accusers. Rather, *they* became the accused, facing a mob whose judging faces bore a close resemblance to their own. Thus they became brothers to the woman. The impact of Jesus' act points out the value of taking another's role.

Role playing is accomplished when a person takes upon himself the life situation of another and attempts to see things from the inside. It is not easy to see life with the eyes of another. To do this we must "sit in his chair," "wear his shoes," or "walk his mile with his aching feet."

A special value of role playing is its ability to show us who we are. The gospel becomes an abstract set of facts to be learned unless the learner can get some perspective on himself, on his needs and behavior, and can connect the truth of the gospel to that perspective.

> Oh wad some power the giftie gie us
> To see oursels as others see us!

Doing this, however, would give us only a partial picture of ourselves. Others see the external; we are required to look deeply into ourselves.

In role playing an individual may come to know another deeply and also to know himself deeply. The two acts may be one, for the New Testament concept of oneness in the spirit involves accepting life from a personal perspective and at the same time making allowances for others.

How can we set the stage for this to happen? Grace Levit and Helen Jennings, in *How to Use Role Playing*,[1] briefly outline the steps in the role-playing process as follows:

Define the Problem: Much of what we say about sorrow and suffering is not real, but just so much pious talk. Many persons have experienced death and suffering and have valuable insights and contributions to make if opportunity is given to them. Role playing will help others test the reality of their own insights.

The first step is to define the problem to be used in the role playing. The focus should be on a problem that is of interest to the whole group. The general subject matter is dictated by the theme before the class. But specific role playing relating to the subject should be chosen by the group. For example, after a study of a particular biblical

[1] Adult Education Association of the U.S.A., 1956.

idea, such as keeping faith in the face of death and bereavement, the class may be broken into groups to discuss life problems related to the idea. The question, To what particular situations does this idea speak? may stimulate the small groups to list such problems.

Choose the situation: From this list the small group may choose one that seems to speak to the needs and interests of the whole group. The situation should give a clear picture of how the biblical idea relates to the human situation. Painful personal situations in the lives of specific individuals within the group should be avoided. This, of course, should not exclude those situations that lie within the common experience of the whole group and are volunteered by a person as personal experience.

An adequate ministry to the bereaved is seldom achieved in the church. A physician's wife told her pastor that she simply could not visit in the homes where death had occurred. She was embarrassed by the fact that she did not know what to say, and in fact she became so emotional she could not talk. Her problem is not unlike the feeling of inadequacy many people have in visiting the bereaved. Probably some people in your group would like help in such Christian service.

Choosing characters: The work group should move now to deciding what characters are needed to play the situation.

"What do you say and how do you act when you visit the bereaved?" With this question the group could have volunteers act out such a situation. After the situation has been properly described, with identification of the bereaved and the ministering person, the group will discuss and act out the scene. Of course, the leader will need to plan the situation in advance. He should describe the situation to be enacted in something of this fashion: Mrs. Ansby is the wife of a small-town physician who goes calling on a neighbor and his wife who have lost a son in military combat. Mrs. Ansby is nervous, emotional, and does not know what to say after she arrives.

When the characters are chosen and described, the individuals in the work group should assume the character roles. Generally, care should be taken to be sure that persons are not cast in roles that are characterized by their own personal problems. Such exposure can be dangerous.

Preparing the audience: While the volunteers are getting "in character," the leader will prepare the group by suggesting specific points to watch for in the role playing. Sometimes it is best to give the audience some "listening questions" before the actual playing of the situation. Questions such as the following will give some motivation for depth analysis: What about this is similar to situations you have known? How realistic is the situation? In what ways do you agree or disagree with the solution?

Presentation: Now the work groups are ready to act out the situation. There is no script in role playing as there is in formal drama. Instead, the characters give spontaneous interpretations in action and word.

Some groups will find it helpful to stop the action at specific points for discussion. Role playing involving a presentation of a situation followed by a solution will readily lend itself to a break in action before the solution is presented. Class members may be asked to decide how they think the solution will or should be developed. A quick one-to-one conversation between people sitting side by side will prove valuable in involving the audience. After the members have had an opportunity to talk, the action should resume as planned.

The learning cycle is not complete at this point. The class may be divided into groups of five to eight for analysis of the role playing, using the listening questions, along with any other questions raised during the break in action. Finally, reports of new ideas, insights, and observations need to be made to the class.

Alan Klein has stated four major uses for role playing:

1. To stimulate discussion.
2. To train in skills.
3. To train in sensitivity and acquire insight so as to solve social and human relations problems.
4. To deal effectively with certain emotional problems that block group productivity.[2]

As with any other procedure, there are hazards to avoid. One of the most frequent mistakes is to force role playing into a rigid time schedule. Do not use it if you are pressed for time. This is not to suggest that role playing always takes a lot of time—just that its effectiveness depends on a relaxed group and proper evaluation.

Failure often results from poor atmosphere. Role playing calls for a warm, easy, accepting atmosphere, with free-

[2] From *Role Playing in Leadership Training and Group Problem Solving* (New York: Association Press, 1956), p. 131.

dom to discuss, differ, explore, and learn. The attitude of the leader is a major factor in the kind of atmosphere prevailing in the group.

Use role playing sparingly, and never as a novelty device. It is not entertainment but a technique for stimulating and training the group. Avoid a highly complex situation, for the action should be spontaneous, with little preparation and no script.

Brainstorming

For some time business, industry, government, the armed services, and educational institutions have used a method popularly known as brainstorming. It is sometimes called "idea inventory." The effectiveness of this procedure has been demonstrated in improving products and in planning programs. It provides an excellent means of prompting the spontaneous expression of ideas in people's minds.

Webster's Third New International Dictionary says that to brainstorm is "to practice a conference technique by which a group attempts to find a solution for a specific problem by amassing all the ideas spontaneously contributed by its members." Simply put, it means to use the brain to storm a problem. The aim is to pile up a quantity of alternative ideas.

In its freest form, this learning process encourages group

members to propose any idea that comes to mind without fear of criticism, laughter, ridicule, or any of the other ways in which creative and imaginative thinking is usually squelched in a group. Christians should practice the brainstorming technique more, since it requires the ability to accept, value, and share every person's individual thinking —a goal serious Christians should hope to attain.

First, this is a technique for discovering the range of information, opinion, creativity, and imagination within the group. Brainstorming helps stretch the group members toward a wider perspective for considering a topic.

Second, brainstorming allows a group to explore every conceivable avenue for study and action relating to the topic under consideration.

Third, brainstorming can function as a means for creating a mood of openness in a group learning situation. The very process conveys to every member a willingness to hear all that is being said, to welcome the contribution of every person's ideas and thoughts, and the need for receiving every member's thoughts if the group is to function effectively.

Fourth, brainstorming encourages persons to value their own thinking more highly. When our ideas are laughed at or our suggestions ignored, we tend to be more hesitant in expressing ourselves thereafter. Each person should be encouraged to make his full contribution to the group.

Alex F. Osborn, one of the early developers of brainstorming, suggests four basic rules:

1. Criticism is ruled out. Adverse judgment of ideas must be withheld until later.

2. "Freewheeling" is welcomed. The wilder the idea, the better; it is easier to tame down than to think up.
3. Quantity is wanted. The greater the number of ideas the more the likelihood of winners.
4. Combination and improvement are sought. In addition to contributing ideas of their own, participants should suggest how ideas of others can be turned into better ideas or how two or more ideas can be joined into still another idea.[1]

These seem to sum up the basic ground rules for using this method. If this is to be an effective procedure, the group must agree to defer judgment of the ideas and to seek as many ideas as the group can generate. Some of the group may have difficulty doing this in the beginning, since most people are accustomed to evaluating their thoughts prior to expression rather than allowing a creative flow of ideas and then evaluating them.

The versatility of brainstorming makes it most helpful as a leadership procedure. It may be used on almost any kind of problem—just so it is a specific, not general, problem and can be presented in a simple form. A long, complex problem or question should be redefined so that it is particular and simple. Likewise, this procedure can be used with almost any size group.

Once the basic purposes of brainstorming are understood, the techniques for using it are easy to apply. Only two things are needed: a means of keeping track of every

[1] *Applied Imagination* (New York: Charles Scribner's Sons, rev. ed. 1957), p. 84.

idea presented during the discussion, and an understanding of the role of the group leader.

Have one person write key idea phrases on a chalkboard or wall chart, thumbtack paper strips to a corkboard, or otherwise create a written record that is visible to the total group as the process continues. An indispensable part of the brainstorming process is the interaction of minds and the stimulation that takes place in every mind as seemingly unrelated new ideas are heard and seen.

The role of the leader in a brainstorming session is not to lead so much as to make certain that every contribution receives its share of attention. Watch carefully for the various visible signs a person gives in advance of making a contribution, especially his first suggestion in the session. Sometimes there is a change of expression in the face, a shifting in the chair, or an opening of the mouth without saying anything.

The leader also must help the person writing down the ideas to phrase the idea properly, seizing upon the essential idea rather than using excess words, rephrasing for clarity and conciseness, and restating in more commonly understood language. Repeat the new wording to the one who gives the idea to be sure it expresses what he has in mind. Take time to work out essential understanding, but *avoid discussing the merits of the idea.*

In a brainstorming session everyone has a contribution to make to the discussion, including the leader. Sometimes it is helpful for the leader to offer a few opening directions, such as samples of possible far-out ideas on the topic. But he moves quickly to the role of average group member.

Ways of using the results of a brainstorming session

49

should be planned carefully in advance, so that these can be shared with the group before they even begin brainstorming. If a project is to be undertaken, the questions to be answered by brainstorming are *how? with what leadership? by what procedure?* After the brainstorming session, when can the group expect some action upon their ideas, and who will take the action? Is there a need for further exploration of a difficult topic, such as race relations, husband-wife relations, or parent-child relations? If there is need for further study, how can those in charge of it select and condense the material generated by the brainstorming session?

The group will, of course, discard the unusable ideas when they get to the point of evaluation. Even this can be an enjoyable, lively experience. Care should be exercised so that no person's ideas are belittled, for such will prove detrimental to future brainstorming experiences.

In the evaluation the leader will make sure the ideas are clearly stated and duplications noted. Out of all the ideas presented, the most promising ones are selected by the group. At this point the group should look carefully at all the ideas. This is the point when they become concerned with the quality of ideas they have produced. Hard thinking centered upon the evaluation of alternatives is required.

Aside from the primary results of brainstorming, there are some very fine by-products. Usually morale is improved, initiative is increased, and personal development is encouraged. Groups or individuals that tend to stagnate and fail to grow will find this to be a stimulus to improve.

Paraphrasing

How great a human faculty is the ability to translate thoughts from one medium of expression to another! The linquist exercises this art when he expresses meanings in a language different from the original. He does this so that persons may find them understandable.

Grasping an idea depends on both a person's ability to understand the words used to express the idea and his ability to relate the words and the thoughts to his own experience. But the thoughts may be expressed in another language, or in the hearer's own language in words not familiar to him. Therefore the linguist translates and the educator paraphrases.

Paraphrasing and translating are not done in an attempt to change meaning. As a matter of fact, if the meaning is changed the artisan has betrayed his craft. The purpose is to express the meaning of the passage in a way that will give clarity and broader understanding.

Although paraphrasing is more frequently thought of in connection with Scripture passages, it need not be limited to such use. One of the most effective procedures for helping a group dig out the meaning of a difficult theological or philosophical idea would be to have them paraphrase a paragraph on the subject. Misunderstandings and lack of clarity show up quickly in such an exercise, when several versions of the same passage are read aloud.

Restatement: Many groups have found a restatement of Scripture to be a helpful learning procedure. Rewriting a passage, taking care to use none of the original words of the text, will yield many new understandings. If group members rewrite or paraphrase a Scripture passage, they should be given ample opportunity to discuss the product and to explore the additional insights and understandings gained in this way.

Evaluation of paraphrases may be approached with questions such as these: Which words have been understood differently by the various members of the group? Are there personal reasons for differing interpretations? What new insights have been expressed?

Circular response: A method of teaching known as circular response may be adapted to paraphrasing. Individuals sitting in a circle may be given a scriptural statement by the leader and asked to restate the idea in other words. Starting with the person to the right of the leader and moving around the circle, each must restate the original in his own words, but he may not do it in the same way as the person before him has done. When all have spoken, the group discussion may revolve around the adequacy of the interpretations. (This method is more useful for groups of five to eight persons than for larger groups.)

Charting: The Ecumenical Institutes have found the charting method of paraphrase a useful tool for depth understanding of concepts presented by writers of theology and philosophy. This method of paraphrasing may be used to develop a summary statement of the writer's thought.

The first step is to read the material paragraph by paragraph. After the reading of each paragraph the student is asked to write the meaning of it in one sentence (or one phrase if possible). After all the paragraphs have been covered, the next step is to write the meaning of all the sentences into one statement. This method will not, of course, give a statement covering all facets of knowledge involved in the material. Thorough study and clearer understanding of the material is the purpose of using this procedure.

A chart of the paragraphs may be produced by a flow chart showing the sentences or phrases from the paragraphs flowing into the one summary statement. This will show more clearly the relationship of the ideas that have been incorporated in the summary.

Tools for paraphrasing: In paraphrasing Scripture a variety of translations of the Bible will be helpful. These might include J. B. Phillips' *New Testament in Modern English;* The New English Bible; *Good News for Modern Man—The New Testament in Today's English Version;* Revised Standard Version of the Bible.

A good dictionary and a thesaurus will provide word meanings and synonyms that will be useful in paraphrasing.

Paraphrasing in lesson preparation: In your reading of other resources you may have found an account of an incident or a meaningful passage that you wish to share with your group. Writing out a paraphrase of the material will help you clarify your thinking on the matter and will make it possible to share these ideas in your own words.

Creative Writing

Writing a story or a letter requires the writer to stand within the shoes of the one to whom or about whom he is writing. This is true even if the writer is writing about himself. When a person stands outside his life and observes objectively his own acts and behavior, he is likely to see a different personality than the one he usually conjures up as "myself." Writing about the experiences of another person leads the writer into a fruitful area of communication. It requires him to become sensitive to the other person's life situation.

But the value of writing and organizing for writing does not end here. This creativity has a massive by-product. The writer may be able to see in the experience of his subject some solutions that will be helpful to him. Or he may be able to use the life experiences of his subject as a trial-and-error testing ground.

The usefulness of this kind of experience becomes even more apparent when we evaluate it in terms of "learning at the intersection." Visualize two streets coming together at an intersection. One of the streets we can label "the gospel," that which is true and unchanging. The other we can label "life situation," that which must change constantly. Where these two intersect, Christian education can take place. When the gospel is allowed to clarify and redirect the life situation of an individual, a new person is born.

But unless that person can find some way to help define himself, to know who he is, the change made possible through encounter with the gospel may not occur for him. Clearly, then, the value and purpose of creative writing is chiefly in its ability to help the learner know who he is and what his life situation means. Let us therefore look at some possible uses of creative writing in the process of group and individual learning.

Transposing a biblical story is one way of taking the biblical material out of the historical and placing it in the present. When music is transposed, it is played in a different key. The melody and chord structure remain the same, but the sound is higher or lower, according to the new key. This is what happens when the characters of a biblical story are changed to contemporary persons. The process does not change the basic issues to which the Scripture speaks, but it does make the story sound different.

Another form of writing that is very useful in small-group discussion is *finishing an open-ended story*. This procedure involves taking a given situation or series of facts and developing a conclusion or solution to the problems described. One group worked with this method for two weeks. After having studied some of the concepts of the biblical writers, groups of three were given situations involving conflict. They were asked to write a three-paragraph story that told of the conflict and the events leading to a solution in the life of the characters in the situation. The leader held the stories until the next session, and at that time groups of three again came together to write endings to the stories. It was so arranged that an individual did not work the second week on the story he began the first week. The stories were read to the whole class and used to prepare a flow chart showing how the ideas of the biblical writer were related to contemporary life situations.

Letter writing can be a very useful kind of creative writing. A leader or committee might allow the total class to help see the goals of the group by having them answer a letter containing a certain number of questions about "goal setting." These letters could be written by the members at the beginning of a unit or series. If these were held until the conclusion of the unit, they could be compared to a second letter the group members are asked to write at that time. This would enable the group to evaluate its own progress.

Perhaps the most useful letter-writing exercises are those in which individuals are asked to write to themselves. One group was asked to write letters to themselves explaining the material they had just discussed and how it should change their way of living during that week. The leader of the group mailed these letters so they would be received near the end of that week. Of course, the natural question raised in the minds of the class members was, Have I done this week what I decided I would do?

One group found it helpful to have writing partners. Each week members took time to write their partners, giving an interpretation of the material of the previous session. Thus each person had the benefit of his partner's insights as well as his own study.

Creative writing has endless possibilities for making the "gospel learned about" into the "gospel acted out." The writer's reaction when he sees his thoughts on paper may even create a desire to change.

Space Carving

Freedom and responsibility are two aspects of our nature which need constant examination. We must live responsibly, that is, in response to God's giving us the freedom of choices. For the process of testing to be a learning experience, we can use a technique called *space carving*.

Let one person at a time be given a cubic block of space for himself and his use. The space might be in the center of the group circle or at one end of the room or even on a raised platform or stage. The instructions are for him just to take this block of space and do with it as he wishes. He is to carve out an expression of himself, his thinking, feelings, desires, hates—whatever he wishes to do.

What can we do with the block of space? How do we express our concerns, ideas, feelings, and fears? It might be helpful to see the learning experience in terms of four areas of searching we are engaged in each day.

First is the search for *personal meaning and identity*. The major question of growing toward maturity is, Who am I? From this flow the questions, How can I be what I want to be? How can I best relate to others, especially in marriage? and, How does my job help or hurt my being me? For the adult, the questions of identity include adjusting to the regular changes or stages of life, especially the losing of loved ones as they grow up, leave home, marry, or die.

Space carving may be used in the following ways to express these experiences. Acting out a question or experience without speaking (pantomime) requires extra effort of expression and movement. Some will find that talking out loud (monologue) or to others (dialogue) aids in the search. A mirror might be used as one talks, to look at one's reflection, seeking to learn what he can. Or the search might be in the form of religious experiences such as prayer, head bowed or kneeling, in a "conversation" with God about the meaning of life.

Second is the search for *understanding*. We seek to understand ourselves and others and to have them understand us. More importantly, we seek understanding of the world we live in and how we fit into the fabric of experiences. To express this search we might have some other group member enter our space and freely tell us what he sees in us, how he thinks we see ourselves, or answer our questions along these lines. Then we can respond in action.

Third is the search for *communication*. We never express ourselves as clearly as we think we do, nor do we receive the communication efforts of others as they would like for us to receive them. Therefore, we engage constantly in a process of testing and clarification.

To test communication we might demonstrate the problem with a game: Whisper information from one person to the next until it comes to the last person. Then repeat the process with each person saying aloud what he thought had been said to him and what he said to the next person.

A special communication problem for many people relates to the Bible. One might use his space-carving experience to demonstrate the different meanings possible for Scripture passages by using several different translations. Paul's great exposition on the nature and meaning of human death and resurrection (I Cor. 15) might be more meaningful if J. B. Phillips' *The New Testament in Modern English* is read, rather than the King James Version.

Fourth is our *search for others*. This goes beyond the effort to make contact with them and to understand them. Our life is a search for genuine and meaningful relationships with others. As John Donne said, "No man is an island."

This is an especially significant area for spacing-carving activity. Diagraming relationships—how they begin, change, develop, and cease—by drawings or by verbally describing them can bring understanding of the processes we engage in. An honest portrayal of what we seek in other people is possible. We can invite them into our "space" and show how we value and need them.

Our goal in space carving is to create an experience in the responsible use of freedom. Such action requires both our own honesty and our willingness to accept the honesty of others. Space carving can assist members of a church school class, who think they know and understand each other, to realize there is always much more to learn about themselves and others.

Space carving requires an opening of personality which some persons do not have. The group leader who plans to use space carving should carefully watch for negative reactions and be prepared to help such persons grow in the experience.

Using Printed Resources

Until recent years, the printed word had been considered the only respectable medium for Christian education. With the revolution in communication brought about by television, fear arose that reading would go out of style. But it has not. Books—especially paperbacks—are the most easily acquired and most portable educational tools.

The gospel, to be meaningful to adults now, must be understood in relation to the ethical problems of work and politics, the personal relationships in families, and the value conflicts in civic groups. Such real confrontation requires use of materials that reveal directly the depths of conflict and concern in these areas. For such material we must turn to creative artists, theorists, and investigators of life in the world. To their contributions we add new approaches to use of the Bible.

Thus all the procedures in this section are designed to assist in the confrontation of the world with the good news that God is at work in this world.

Guided Study with Adults

When a student confronts a printed page, how should he proceed to study it? What method can a teacher use in guiding his class in the study of a printed text? Are there any plans of guided study that will ensure the fruitful use of printed material? Even today, when filmstrips, motion pictures, and television are so common and are so easily available to the church school, printed materials such as magazines and books remain the primary curriculum resource.

Yet the problem facing many church school classes is that the material in the student periodical is not read. Our hope that adult students will read and prepare for class sessions has been disappointed again and again. However, some teachers have found that students are willing to read and to be guided in their reading *during the class session itself.* It may be that we should experiment more than we have with guided reading and guided study within the class period. One solution to the problem may be to add half an hour or more to the length of the class sessions and to use that extra time for the reading and preparation that good discussion and good learning demand but that we are not getting from our students outside the class period.

Teachers, therefore, need a method that will guide classes in using their study material. The method presented here may be used with books, chapters from a book, church school periodicals, or printed sermons. It may be used, in fact, with any printed resource in the church school.

I shall describe this method in five steps. In order to be effective, guided study must be followed step by step in the order given here. These verbs describe the steps: *read and outline, recall, interpret, evaluate,* and *apply.*

Step one: Every student should have a copy of the text to be studied. Ask every student to number the paragraphs in the text 1, 2, 3, and so forth. Each paragraph should have one number. No paragraph, however short, should be un-numbered. The entire article or chapter to be studied on a given day should be numbered in this fashion. Ask the students to read the article from beginning to end one time simply to get the overall idea of the article. Then ask them to read the article a second time in order to discover the main point in each paragraph.

Each student should have a sheet of paper numbered in a way that corresponds to the numbered paragraphs in the text. For example, if the chapter chosen has fifty paragraphs, there should be fifty numbers on the student sheet. *The main idea of each paragraph should be stated in one sentence and written on the numbered sheet.* Each paragraph and each sentence will be identified by the numbers they bear.

After every paragraph has been condensed with a summary sentence, the students should read their sentences and group them into blocks of thought. A chapter that has fifty paragraphs will produce fifty key sentences; these key sentences may then logically fall into five, six, seven, or eight groups of ideas. When these are grouped together by brackets or some marking, the chapter will be outlined.

When first used, this method may seem tedious and pedantic. Some students may feel that it is artificial and unnecessary. They may react against giving so much careful attention to what is read. However, a method such as this usually can treat the writer of the material with justice. If a chapter or a book has been prepared with thought and care, it should be assimilated with thought and care. If the chapter has anything significant to say, then the reader is responsible for discovering *accurately* what in fact it does say.

Reading as suggested, however, is only the beginning of guided study. What should a class do next?

Step two is to recall what the writer has said. If a class is going to use a printed resource, their first responsibility is to *state to one another* what the writer has said. They should use their key sentences and the outlines they have prepared. Perhaps one person can chart on a chalkboard his way of grouping the ideas in the chapter or in the lesson. The class may agree on a sentence that best summarizes each paragraph as they compare the sentences they have written. The basic meaning of each paragraph will be discovered. As these sentences are written on the chalkboard and grouped into blocks of thought, the structure and fundamental content of the chapter will emerge.

At this stage the class *should not evaluate* what has been said. At this point there should be as little interpretation as possible. *Interpretation* (step three) and *evaluation* (step four) *should be delayed until the ideas presented by the text are understood in their own language and their own context.* If the class begins to react to the basic ideas and to evaluate these ideas before they are understood, the evaluation will almost certainly be unjust.

Step three is interpretation. (Evaluation is still to be postponed.) In this step of the guided study the class members try to say in other words what the writer has said, but they are not to decide at this point if they reject or accept his ideas. They are not to decide if what he says is true or untrue, Christian or unchristian, pleasant or painful. *Evaluation must be postponed until understanding is achieved.*

At this stage in the guided study, the class should be trying to test its understanding of the writer by saying in a new way what the writer has said. If we can say something in only one set of words, we probably have words and not an idea. But if an idea is truly ours, we can recast it into a variety of words and state it in a variety of ways.

Step four, then, is evaluation. Now the students are invited to give their own personal reactions. They place their experience up against the experience of the writer. They say whether they think he is right or wrong, helpful or unhelpful, clear or mysterious, Christian or unchristian, and why. At this point also the writer's ideas should be tested by Scripture. To compare what he has written to Scripture is essential, but it is evaluation and should be postponed until after recall and interpretation.

The teacher using this method should outline in advance the steps to be followed, explain the rationale for each step, explain why the steps come in the order they come, and explain how they move in a logical fashion from an appropriation of the text to an application of it. If the students are assured in this way that their personal thoughts are to be accepted at step four, they will find it much easier to fulfill steps one, two, and three. If the students do not know the framework of the whole method, and if they do not know that a time has been planned for them to react, then they may find it impossible and undesirable to withhold their evaluations until the proper time.

This method assumes that the class is studying something that has a substantial content, in which every paragraph counts. Material that is thin, poorly written, or frivolous is not worth the meticulous approach this method demands. Therefore, a class that is serious about guided reading and guided study must be serious enough to select material that is solid and perhaps more difficult than that they have used before.

Step five is application. The chapter has been read once, read a second time, and outlined. The class has agreed upon an outline and has placed it on the chalkboard. Together they have interpreted and restated the original ideas of the author and evaluated them. The class members are ready now to use in their own lives the principles they have learned.

There is no general way to say what step five will be like. It should be the step that brings the ideas of the writer into immediate, creative relationship with the situation of the student and the class. Commitment, personal transformation, mission to the world are the purposes of study in the church. Therefore each unit of study should end with some plan for action, service, or testing of what has been learned. This is the climax of this whole process.

Tracing an Idea Through the Bible

Frank Spline sat on the edge of his chair as he always did in a discussion when he was on the defensive. "Women have no business trying to be pastoral ministers," he argued.

"But," said Martha Sellers, "women could bring qualities to the office that men couldn't."

"As it says in the Bible," answered Frank sharply, "woman shall remain in the home."

Martha was quiet. Frank always got the last word by quoting the Bible. How did he know so much about the Bible? Then she felt a hunch. She leaned forward and said, "Where does it say *that* in the Bible, Frank?"

Frank started to answer, but no words came. "Why . . . why, I don't know for sure, but what difference does it make? I know it says it."

"I'd like to know," said Martha, "so I can read more about it."

But, interestingly enough, when a search was made for Frank's quotation, it could not be found. Further, they discovered most of Frank's the-Bible-says statements were not biblical at all, but were distortions. From then on Frank had to watch his quotations. In fact, Martha became the "Bible-idea watchdog." Through her efforts the class learned to trace an idea through the Bible and thus to use it more accurately.

Many a class discussion has floundered because members did not take the responsibility to use the Bible and its ideas with precision. We must recognize that the Bible is not a simple document and is not easy to understand.

Find the big ideas in the Bible: Many persons feel that the abundance of detail in the Bible is confusing. "Who cares who begat whom?" asked one frustrated layman. How can one break through the mass of details?

Finding the big idea and tracing it is one way. For instance, one basic idea of the Bible is love. What does it mean to love? How many persons do you know who dismiss this question with, "Am I my brother's keeper?" There are other key ideas too, like the ideas of God, of man, of immortality.

To find the ideas and trace them with accuracy, most persons need tools. One valuable reference is Harry Emerson Fosdick's *A Guide to Understanding the Bible,* in which he does what I have just described.

Other tools are needed: one or more translations of the Bible, one good Bible commentary, a notebook in which you can keep your own ideas as they evolve, and an open eye for books of biblical interpretation as they come off the presses. This number of books is no more extensive than the collection of cookbooks or furniture repair manuals found in many homes. As much time spent with the Bible "tools" as with other how-to-do-it manuals will produce a working relationship with the great ideas of the Bible.

Use the method in class work: But will a church school class take time to trace an idea in the Bible? The first step would be to get the class to adopt the policy that it will never consider a biblical idea without approaching it in depth. Then when the time comes to see what the Bible says, appoint a committee of two or three to do the spadework in advance and report their findings to the total group. This can be done with each unit; or two committees could work within one unit if there are many ideas to research.

Another approach would be to assign the same task to two different committees. Let each trace the idea independently and then present the results to the whole class in the form of a panel.

Occasionally a class could make use of a resource person to trace a complex idea through the Bible. For instance, the biblical concept of work may be more than the ordinary person can handle, but a resource person with some experience might perform a valuable service by going into the idea in detail. A warning: This procedure can be deadly unless it involves class members. The members might be divided into listen-discuss groups. After the presentation each group can discuss what was said and formulate questions about it. When the total group assembles, the questions can be put to the resource person.

Knowing when to probe a biblical idea in the context of a unit of study is important. The class leader sometimes has this skill, or any member may know when to say, "Let's take a good look at the Bible and see what it says on this idea." Poor timing results in forcing biblical material into a discussion just because "this is a church school class and we must study the Bible somehow." Biblical ideas introduced under this latter impetus are quickly dismissed. However, the Bible becomes a real resource when its relevant ideas are discovered and used by class members to deepen their understanding of life.

Comparing Bible Stories with Novels

Christian education is based on the understanding that to be integrated, whole, unified, the personality must be motivated by an ideal higher than any that can be accomplished immediately. The Christian understands that ideal to be the life of Christ. His life was centered upon two principal goals: to understand and do the will of God, and to show love and respect for God's children.

These two goals make up our concept of Christian life; that is, we live under God's care and love, and therefore our life must be one of service to mankind. Through Christian education an individual gains an understanding of this concept and what it means in the everyday events of this life.

To communicate to another person that our concept of life is to be in his service, we must stand in his place. We must be able to imagine what life means to that person. We may develop many sentiments about serving, but most of these will be wasted unless we can see what they would mean in the life of another.

The novel, used as an educational tool, will give us an opportunity to develop this understanding. It has been hard for Christian educators to understand the power of the novel to illustrate the gospel at work. Often novels deal with situations some Christians may find taboo as subjects for discussion. Such situations may well exist in a Christian's life, but he is unwilling to admit to others that they do. A serious study of the novel can lead us to a new honesty about our real problems. And it may give us some insights about other persons.

Biblical novels: "And Pilate asked him, 'Are you the King of the Jews?' And he [Jesus] answered him, 'You have said so.' " (Mark 15:2) Why did Pilate phrase his question to Jesus in this way? Did he really have some question about the authenticity of Jesus? Or did his humanitarian instinct make him want to avoid bloodshed if possible? These questions may be the key to a new understanding of the power of Jesus before Pilate.

Lloyd C. Douglas, in chapter six of *The Robe,* presents one view of the situation.

"The witnesses said he [Jesus] acted, at the Temple, as if it were his own personal property . . . . At old man Annas' house, I'm bound if he didn't act as if he owned the place. At Caiaphas' palace, everybody was on trial—but this Jesus! He was the only cool man in the crowd at the Insula. He owns that, too. Pilate felt it, I think. One of the witnesses testified that Jesus had professed to be a king. Pilate leaned forward, looked him squarely in the face, and said, "Are you?" Mind, sir, Pilate didn't ask him, "Did you say you were a king?" He said, "Are you?" And he wasn't trying to be sarcastic, either."

A group could engage in some useful grappling with the question: Is this account true to Pilate's feelings as presented in the Scripture?

An expansion of this method of study may open many doors. For instance, one group decided to study the Roman reaction to Jesus by using the entire scene from which Paulus' speech was taken. A planning committee prepared a chart of the specific incidents in the life of Christ spoken of by Paulus and his commander Marcellus. The committee also selected two men to read the dialogue of Paulus and Marcellus.

After the presentation of the chart and the dialogue, the group was broken into committees of about five persons each. Each committee was asked to write a short, informal drama using the two characters Marcellus and Paulus. Each committee was given an opportunity to present its drama, and this was followed by total group discussion.

The nonbiblical novel: The Christian faith must be understood as speaking directly to the rawest experiences of life. After all, much of human life is "raw." This rawness presents our biggest problem. The part of our life most needing the ministry of the faith is that part which we often think is too crude to hear the gospel.

For some, the writing of Albert Camus may be useful. One work that lends itself to a comparison with elements in the life and teaching of Jesus is *The Plague*. A list of traditional words used to interpret Jesus' life could form an outline for group study. For instance, where do you see the following symbols in *The Plague:* sin, salvation, crucifixion, grave, resurrection?

To present a broader understanding of the contemporary meaning of these traditional Christian concepts, several novels might be compared.

Some novels for comparison: biblical novels: *Dear and Glorious Physician,* by Taylor Caldwell; *The Source,* by James A. Michener.

Nonbiblical novels: *The Brothers Karamazov,* by Feodor Dostoevsky; *The Sound and the Fury,* by William Faulkner; *The Fall,* by Albert Camus.

Play Cuttings for Reading and Discussion

For many years drama was alienated from the life and ministry of the church. This is a surprising historical fact, for a study of the history of drama reveals that it had its roots in religion.

Furthermore, redemption may be thought of as divine "drama." There is a beginning, a middle, and an end: Creation, Crucifixion, and the Last Judgment. Christian education must be seen as a means of redemption or it has no place in the ministry of the church.

And thus Christian education may offer involvement not only in *belief* in the drama of Creation, Crucifixion, and the Last Judgment, but also in the *method* of drama—an instrument of redemption. As God is seen to have worked his plan of redemption of mankind in a divine historical drama, so a man may gain insights into his own redemption from a human drama—a play that deals with the elements of redemption.

Christian education has been on the growing edge of the recent renewal of theology, which has often found expression in drama. This renewal can take the church into the depths of human existence where it should be.

Since the use of drama within the church has also experienced a recent renewal, religious drama of adequate quality is more generally found in recent writings. Still, choosing a play for use in Christian education is not an easy matter. To be of value in Christian education, a play must speak to the real problems of the audience and should allow each viewer to identify with some aspect of its presentation.

When preparing to use a play or a cutting, the planning

committee or leader should have studied the play in advance to be sure the cutting is adequate for the subject.

Characters should be selected in advance and given the script to study. Usually the characters need to get together beforehand to read this material, but when no acting is involved the characters may not need to rehearse at all.

Preparing the audience properly to hear the reading is a very important aspect of the presentation. The following factors should be clearly described to the group before the reading: the place of the action, the time of the action, the relationship of this section to the whole play, and the characters' relationships to one another.

Cuttings of plays may be compared directly with biblical stories and concepts. If this is done, a reading of the play or scene should be done in class *after* an introduction to the biblical material involved. Group discussion should follow, aimed at understanding how the drama writer is interpreting the Scriptures.

One of the best series of plays for this kind of study is published in *The Man Born to Be King,* by Dorothy L. Sayers. These plays were originally written for radio broadcasting. The entire series is a cycle on the life of Jesus. Good directions for cutting are given in the manuscript.

Plays that are not biblical in content and character may speak to some groups. Many recent ones deal with the traditional elements of the faith.

For Heaven's Sake, by Helen Kromer and Frederick Silver,[1] is representative of a group of modern plays that attempts to answer the question of identity. This particular group of dramatic settings deals with the meaning (or lack

[1] (Boston: Baker's Plays, 1961.)

of meaning) of the church and the inadequate relationships of persons inside and outside the church.

Any one of the scenes in this play could be presented as the basic material for a class session. In small groups members could begin by asking how it is related to their own lives: How are we like this character? The groups will not have finished their work until they have also asked the personal question: If we are like this, how do we free ourselves and become new beings?

Other useful plays are *The Sign of Jonah,* by Guenter Rutenborn.[2] A difficult but excellent play, it deals with the mission of the church and our predicament in refusing to meet God's challenges when they come.

Cry, the Beloved Country, by Felicia Komai.[3] An excellent adaptation of Alan Paton's novel of South Africa, it is useful in its entirety, or for a cutting to begin a discussion of race relations.

A Man for All Seasons, by Robert Bolt.[4] This historical drama is about Sir Thomas More of England, whose unwillingness to compromise in his duty to God and the church led to his being beheaded.

Short Stories

Short stories present a vast pageant of people going about the business of living. Since nothing interests us

[2] (Camden, N. J.: Thomas Nelson & Sons, 1960.)

[3] (New York: Friendship Press, 1955.)

[4] (New York: Random House, 1962.)

more than other people—how they live, what they do, what they think and feel—the fictional short story and novel is the favorite recreational reading of millions of Americans.

You can find some of the great authors in inexpensive paperback editions on your newsstand. Pick up *50 Great Stories* or *Short Story Masterpieces,* and you can read Mark Twain, William Faulkner, Ernest Hemingway, James Agee, James Thurber, George Bernard Shaw, and others. One of the most interesting new writers is John Updike. His book *The Same Door* is a fine example of the way an artist with words can probe deeply into the daily dramas of human existence.

Many current national magazines, such as *McCall's, Good Housekeeping, Redbook, Ladies' Home Journal,* and *Atlantic Monthly,* devote part of their space each month to short stories.

Religious publications such as *The Christian Home* and *Together* contain short story features that have a real teaching value. Monthly nondenominational publications such as *Guideposts* and *Dominion* often carry true stories of persons whose lives have been changed by a vibrant faith. Remember also that short stories frequently appear in the regular church school curriculum materials for children and youth. If parents are familiar with this literature, it can be the springboard for family discussions and religious teaching at home.

A good short story is a unique account of fun, adventure, mystery, or love. It spotlights a selected piece of human experience and lifts it up to view. As you read the story, you feel that you have a new understanding of some bit of reality or human emotion. Because it is descriptive of human behavior, it is an ideal teaching tool.

If you do use short stories in teaching, you should read them for maximum understanding. As you read, watch for the following parts of the story:

The opening. Here you pick up information about the time of the story, the location, the cast of characters, the author's point of view, and the mood of the human drama.

The action. The plot may involve definite kinds of conflicts or problems that are resolved at the end; it may carry the reader on toward the outcome either in suspense or in a combination of concern for the characters and uncertainty as to their fate. Some stories, however, simply present a slice of human experience and only give impressions of persons in interaction.

The people. Rarely does the author give a long description of his characters. You pick up bits of information here and there—by what they do, what they say, or what other characters say about them. If they are real people you can see yourself or others in them.

The message. The message may be pointed or subtle. Not all short stories have a message, however; some authors want only to amuse, frighten, or entertain.

Each part of the short story offers an opportunity for launching into some learning experience.

Here are several key suggestions for consideration in the use of short stories:

1. Appropriateness. The story ought to relate to the

theme of the lesson and add some significant content or new approach to the subject under consideration. Sometimes it may provide a provocative opening or an inspiring closing to a learning experience.

2. Advance reading. Before discussing the story the group should either have read it or heard it read.

3. Carefully planned review. Some guide questions could be formulated to help provoke group discussion. A panel of persons could comment on the story, or the leader might make some interpretive remarks about it. He may want to select certain key passages for restudy by the group.

4. Conclusions from the review. The leader or the group should seek to discover new insights or values from this story.

A good example of a short story about a happy marriage is John Updike's "Wife-wooing" in his book *Pigeon Feathers and Other Stories.* Here is an impressionistic view of a satisfying marriage as narrated by a contended husband. A dramatic reading of this story to a group discussing the marriage relationship could provoke considerable comment. Other similar stories can open a whole new world of discovery for persons who use them creatively.

Poetry

The Christian faith and the arts have always been closely linked. Poetry has had a particularly wide influence and played a significant role. It has been used extensively in conveying and expressing the Christian faith and heritage.

Other than commonly accepted poetry, the church has had two sources of poetry: the Bible and the hymnbook. The Book of Psalms represents our largest collection of biblical poetry. Jesus quite frequently quoted from the Psalms. He also used the pattern of the Psalms to express his teachings. For example, in the style of the Psalms he echoed one thought with variation in two other phrases in Matthew 7:7: "Ask, and it will be given you; seek, and you will find; knock, and it will be opened to you."

The hymnbook is a rich source of poetic expressions of Christian faith, struggle, and hope. Classes could profitably use the hymnbook for purposes other than simply singing songs.

How can we use poetry in our study groups? We immediately think of its use in lectures, sermons, devotionals. Surely, though, it has a use greater than that of illustrative material. It can be a very fine means of expressing feelings as well as conveying truth and meanings.

Let the group members try their hands at *writing poetry*. Encourage a genuine expression of feeling concerning certain ideas. Choose ideas, events, or matters about which there is great feeling. This will call forth the expression, whether or not it rhymes or is in perfect rhythmic pattern. Do not ask for long poems; short, simple expressions of how they feel, see, or understand are better. You might have them read together a poem that a group member has written.

If you have slides or can *obtain pictures* of great art

masterpieces, use these with poetry and music to assist in creating a vivid, pleasing mood. We need to make use of every means available to create the proper emotional impression. For example, along with poetry about the cross you might use a great artist's conception of the Crucifixion.

There are numerous ways to use *choral speaking* in church groups. Mary Alice Douty has written, "To anyone who loves great literature, the sound of words, and the noble expression of fine thought, choral speaking offers a new experience in understanding and enjoyment." [1] The church has regularly used this method with its litanies and various responses. An imaginative leader will search all means to achieve group participation.

When you use choral speaking be sure you understand and appreciate the message in the material. Look up the pronunciation of every unfamiliar word. Read the piece aloud to the group, using tone quality to stress significant words and phrases. Nothing is more deadly to the poet's message than a monotone. Use stress, pause, and pitch to interpret the message in choral speaking.

Place on newsprint or the chalkboard a poem that speaks to the topic, and ask for *small-group discussion* to discover the meanings. Remind them that a poem can have different meanings for different persons. They are not required to see things alike or think the same thoughts.

Suppose you are dealing with the Atonement or the death of Jesus. After certain facts have been presented, you might uncover from the chalkboard, newsprint, or

[1] *How to Work With Church Groups* (Nashville: Abingdon Press, 1957), p. 141.

poster board the poem "In Thine Own Heart," by Angelus Silesius:

> Though Christ a thousand times
> In Bethlehem be born,
> If he's not born in thee
> Thy soul is still forlorn.
> The cross on Golgotha
> Will never save thy soul,
> The cross in thine own heart
> Alone can make thee whole.

Have them read it aloud in choral reading fashion, then silently. Ask them to share together in groups of three or four what they got from the poem. Place these ideas on the chalkboard to share with the whole group.

Listen to what the people in your class are saying. It will help immensely in guiding them to discover and appropriate the truth and to reach out for changes. Listen to their expression of what poems mean. The effective leader does not impose his personal understandings on the group. It is more important to help them discover for themselves.

Primarily, poetry is used to stimulate thought and to express feelings. It can be very useful in helping persons obtain knowledge, seek meanings, and make changes in attitude and behavior.

C. S. Lewis once defined poetry as a "little incarnation, giving body to what had been before invisible and inaudible." It is also a good way of understanding leadership. The leader's function is to help persons "give body to what had been before invisible and inaudible." [2]

[2] *Reflections on the Psalms* (New York: Harcourt, Brace & World, 1958), p. 5.

Biography

Through biographical study, we can reach back into history into a greater variety of lives and experiences, and cover a wider area of concerns than with learning techniques that focus attention only on the experiences of one or two contemporary persons.

This broader historical perspective provides a basis for developing an overview of a problem. It is possible to look for recurring trends, experiences, reactions, or causes and effects as one studies how two different persons in different times have met the challenges to their life values. The essence of biographical study is to discover the motivation of the person being studied. The motivation may be conscious or unconscious, strong or weak, constant or periodic. The results of such study will indicate levels of commitment, degrees of opportunity, and duration of concern. Learning to recognize these factors can help us identify them as they occur in our own experiences.

A significant characteristic of almost any person who attains sufficient stature to be the subject of a biography is the way in which the person invested his life in others. Booker T. Washington is an example often cited, as are Marie and Pierre Curie, Abraham Lincoln, and John Wesley. The types of people who are subjects of biography include discoverers, servants, saints, and manipulators of systems (administrative, political, or ecclesiastical). Recognition of these characteristics provides a basis for evaluating and relating the biography to current concerns.

When reading a biography, look for the skills needed or acquired for the accomplishments recounted. Are these skills needed today in our situation for the solution of current problems? That is, how dated is the procedure for accomplishing the goals described in the biography? Does a Peace Corps worker or an agricultural missionary face some, or none, of the challenges Booker T. Washington faced? What relationship do Washington's skills have to such contemporary situations? If there is little direct point of contact, the study of a biography may be more of an exercise in reviewing history than in learning useful information.

Biography can direct or divert our attention to or from truly significant understandings. Arnold Zeitlin's *To the Peace Corps, With Love* can be most helpful in learning why American youth are joining this modern missionary force by the thousands while they reject the traditional religious missionary service. Such an understanding is more significant than the various personal experiences Zietlin recounts.

When using biography, one should prepare by asking what issues the biographical subject was caught up in and how they concern us. The Peace Corps is a twentieth-century form of man's response to the need of his fellow-men. To understand how this particular response is different from and similar to earlier movements can be helpful, if the information is carefully used. Another type of response to the demands of life, and another form of literary endeavor revealing this response is *Heroic Heart*, the diary and letters of Kim Malthe-Bruun. Kim was a young Danish seaman who died for freedom at the hands of the Gestapo.

Through the eyes of a participant, it is possible in a limited way to enter the actual experience someone else has had. But the biography, as distinguished from the autobiography, allows for questions of evaluation to be asked. Were the goals sought actually reached? What limitations of time, opportunity, personality, or facilities affected the outcome? Answers to these questions help identify the various factors that might affect one's own involvement and action. For example, Courtney Anderson's biography of Adoniram Judson, *To the Golden Shore,* says in the Foreword:

And there is a final trajectory on a curve only one Navigator can draw, to an intersection only one Navigator can locate.

This One issued a command:

"All power is given unto me in heaven and in earth. Go ye therefore, and teach all nations, baptizing them in the name of the Father, and of the Son, and of the Holy Ghost: Teaching them to observe all things whatsoever I have commanded you: and lo, I am with you alway, even unto the end of the world."

He obeyed it.

The question remains: Why? [1]

Biography provides the learning group with another tool for involving group members in limited but significant ways. The housewife, student, commuter, or retired person may be able to read a biography and make a report but be unable to be involved in other types of learning techniques. A librarian might be able to select and make available a diversified list of biographies and other source material. While the level of involvement may be less than with some other techniques, it can be highly motivating for the person doing the reading.

[1] (Boston: Little, Brown and Company, 1956.)

The goal in using biography as a learning technique is to acquire historical perspective, to identify trends, recurring factors or patterns, and to understand the reasons for specific responses by specific people in specific past situations. As these are reviewed and evaluated, it is probable that new understanding for determining current and future action can be developed. Also, the technique provides for a specific type of involvement of individuals.

Quotations

In rebelling against the use of quotations as "proof text" —both biblical and nonscriptural—some people try never to use quotations, but this is neither possible nor desirable. Reaction to a quotation is our goal, but such reaction needs to be an inquiry into rather than an elimination of information sources.

The quotation is one of the most common learning techniques we use. We like to support any important statement we make with the view of someone else, usually an authority—a person considered to have superior knowledge of the subject.

The quotation can challenge prevailing opinion or statements of prejudice. Since many viewpoints exist on every subject, locating a quotation that can be set against almost any idea expressed in a group is not difficult. Such use of a quotation can force us to open our thinking.

While the use of quotations for support or challenge is frequent, the thoughtful leader or group member will find quotations are helpful for summarizing viewpoints, emphasizing key ideas of typical positions on issues, and sharing the experiences of many other people.

Quotations can be used to define general terms and labels. It is more meaningful to have Jean-Paul Sartre's statements on the meaninglessness of daily life as the basis for a Christian critique than to ask, Who knows what existentialism is? More learning can take place in a group if it assembles statements of the ways people forget God as they live each day than if the group only listens to a lecture on secularism.

Summarizing a group discussion of a book can provide insight into both the author's ideas and those of the group. A "reporter" can read back to the group quotations of key statements of the author and those of several persons in the group. Arrange the latter in a list beginning with those which most nearly agree, continuing on through variations to those which disagree most with the author. The group members will see what their own views are in relation to one another and to an outside source.

Sources of quotations are limitless. Encourage learners to seek many different sources rather than lean on only those that agree or disagree sharply with one viewpoint. Every newspaper is filled with usable quotations. News magazines such as *Newsweek, Time,* and *U.S. News and World Report* are useful. Read carefully feature articles and depth interviews in search of personal statements of belief and experience which can be studied. Radio and television programs are sometimes useful, especially if a tape recording can be made of all or part of a program. Speeches, sermons, lectures, and interviews are possible sources of quotations. Again, consider using a tape recording for accuracy and authenticity. (See pages 122-30.)

Seek out the kinds of quotations that would be useful in a learning situation. The interview is one method of securing information in a useful form. Sometimes a written quotation means more in a learning situation if it is recorded and/or visualized. As long as the reproduction is faithful to the original purpose, intent, and meaning, a quotation can be moved from the print media of books, papers, and magazines to recordings, drawings, graphs, pictures, and films. *Credit always should be given to the original source.*

The quoting of Scripture should not be abandoned. It is proper to ask "What did Jesus say?" or "What was Paul's position?" or "How did the Gospel writers think of man's search for a fuller relationship with God?" In quoting Scripture the same guidelines apply: Reproduce the quotation and source accurately, seek the author's intent, look for the relevance to the issue under consideration, and without prejudice relate the meaning to current experience. Commentaries such as *The Interpreter's Bible* can be especially helpful for finding quotations on biblical passages.

Headlines

The mass communications media not only reflect prevailing standards of society but often have great influence in determining values of the community. An examination of actual headlines in current newspapers and periodicals will be useful in a study of society and Christian and cultural values.

In discussing particular headlines, these questions should be kept in mind: How objective are they? How emotion-laden? What assumptions do they make regarding people's sense of values? Do they reflect the actual content of the article? To what extent do they stimulate questioning, or do they tend to close off further exploration of ideas? What does the headline tell about the writer's system of values?

You will find that certain headlines help communicate spiritual values to the reader. Others are useful in a different way—to serve as examples of how Christian values are being undermined. Sometimes this tendency is almost inevitable (as in the case of war news that undermines the scriptural injunction to "love your enemies").

In other cases, the headline might need to be reworded to make it more representative of the underlying reading material. Sometimes the writer's bias in the wording of headlines is hard to detect, but it may show up quite clearly if you can compare one publication's write-ups against those of another on the same subject.

Headlines may be used in an entirely different way in presentation of church school lessons. The ultimate condensation of lesson content is in the form of the lesson title or headline. These few words are or should be the most important ones in the lesson because of their function of capturing the reader's interest. Their effectiveness with headline-oriented readers will be improved if they are expressed in language similar to that used in contemporary secular publications.

At first some students may be shocked to see biblical subjects introduced in journalese in the present tense, but if it gives them the same sense of immediacy as the newspaper headlines, this should provide an added stimulus to become involved in the "now" significance of ancient spiritual truths. Another plus can be achieved simply by use of alternative phraseology, in line with prevailing Bible commentaries, to help clarify difficult Scripture passages.

Old Testament subjects lend themselves very effectively to headline treatment. For instance, "Gigantic Construction Project Completed in Week" might well have headlined the Genesis story of the earth's creation, if there had been newspapers at the time. The next time this subject is due in your teaching schedule, why not use such a headline in making the assignment? If you have access to an opaque projector, you have an ideal method of projecting such a headline, followed by the Scripture passage, on a screen for all the class to study. Or you may simply copy the headline on newsprint or chalkboard.

Sports fans would surely appreciate the story of David and Goliath under this banner: "Phils Rocked by Rookie for House of David; Hurls One-Hitter Against Giant's Team."

The parables of the New Testament are almost ready-made subjects of headlines. For example, Matthew 13:3-8 should come alive for any rural folk under this heading, which could have come straight out of a farm journal: "Crop Yield Depends on Soil Quality." Such a headline helps focus attention away from the parable's popular nick-name, "parable of the sower," toward a more representative caption, "parable of the soil," which deserves more wide-spread use.

In almost any of the Bible translations, from King James to the present, you find some sort of chapter headings, page captions, or subheadings for groups of verses which help identify them. While these are generally descriptive and useful, they rarely reflect the urgency shown by secular headlines. Your best resource for acquiring a sense of immediacy about your Scripture quotations (and of passing this on to your class) is to develop your own headlines for them. Some sample headlines, with the passages they fit, are listed below:

"Healing of Psycho Causes Stampede of Pigs"—Mark 5:1-20

"For Feasting or Fasting, Jesus and John Are Both Rejected by Hierarchy"—Luke 7:29-34

"Ex 'Call Girl' Loves Jesus Because He Forgave Her" —Luke 7:36-50

To test your group's understanding of the biblical passages you use, let them try writing some headlines. Then examine several by using the questions in the second paragraph of this procedure.

Psychological Studies

Only in recent years have our churches turned to the use of careful scientific research. This use has come about with the awareness that science has enabled us to develop a more accurate analysis of the motives and attitudes of man. Conversations in a seminar or conference room do not always provide answers to probing questions about human behavior. Many of the great riddles in life concerning man's motives and conduct have been resolved through valid psychological and sociological studies.

Curriculum materials for the church school need to be based on valid human needs, which can be more accurately discerned through testing.

The United Presbyterian Church, the Lutheran Church (Missouri Synod), The United Methodist Church, and other denominations, as well as the National Council of Churches, have conducted studies to secure the information they needed in planning and teaching. Leaders of adult study groups can also use such studies to gain new insight into a wide range of human relationships.

Certain guidelines should be followed in order to provide for the maximum use of this information:

Locate the studies well in advance of their use. You can find them in popular magazines, scholarly works, professional journals, and by contacting leaders in the fields of psychology and sociology. Check your public library for references. Call or write some of the teachers in the nearest high school or college for detailed information. These persons might be willing to come to your class in the role of resource persons to explain the studies in detail and to answer questions about their interpretation.

Be clear about the purpose for the use of the study. Is it to add to your presentation of the subject matter? Would it be used as the basis for group discussion? Have you asked class members to review the results to help resolve a conflict of opinion over a certain issue? Depending upon your purpose, you may want to present only the briefest summary of the study or engage in detailed examination.

Present the study in a clear and logical manner. Sometimes this can be done by putting the figures on a graph or chart. You can place the conclusions on newsprint, a blackboard, or a large poster card. Usually a study is presented in four phases: (1) the problem under investigation, (2) the method of research, (3) the problems encountered, and (4) the results and conclusions. Unnecessary detail should be avoided.

Arrange for group reaction to the study. Discussion questions can be presented verbally, listed on a blackboard, or given out on a mimeographed sheet. Organize groups of not over ten persons to react to the study and to report their group opinions. If the group is large and the time short, you might want to handle group comment through a reaction panel of representatives of the total class.

Summarize the total group response. Usually, it is advisable to work with a group recorder, who takes brief notes on the entire discussion and gives a summary at its close. A recorder could give feedback as to whether or not the study was understood by the class members.

One helpful way to gain values from a study of feelings and attitudes is to secure class consent to use a test instrument on themselves. You may purchase easy-to-use inventories from Family Life Publication, Inc., P. O. Box 6725, at Durham, North Carolina. This company publishes a whole series of inexpensive tests with counselor's guides, which could be administered by a minister, a skilled school counselor, or a psychologist. The lists of aids includes these:

A Courtship Analysis, by McHugh.

A Dating Problems Checklist, by McHugh.

A Marriage Adjustment Form, by Burgess

A Marriage Prediction Schedule, by Burgess.

A Marriage Role Expectation Inventory, by Dunn.

A Religious Attitudes Inventory, by Crane and Coffer.

These instruments should not be imposed on a class or used against their will. The results should be kept confidential. A general summary of the results would satisfy the need for information about the completed test scores without identifying anyone. The use of these tests, however, could be a powerful means of pinpointing problem areas for class members. It may lift up key concerns that the members should deal with frankly in group discussion. It may also help some persons seek a counselor and face crucial problems they have evaded.

Sociological and psychological studies are effective and unique tools for a learning group. We should employ them more often because they provide us with depth insight into the meaning of human behavior.

Government Publications

In looking for resources for study of a particular subject, we often overlook a source of factual materials based on competent studies which are inexpensive—publications of the various departments and bureaus of the United States government. The mailing address from which such publications—on a myriad of subjects—are available is: Superintendent of Documents, U. S. Government Printing Office, Washington, D.C. 20502.

An *illustration of the availability and value of those resources* is provided in the following discussion of the use of documents relating to the subject of disarmament.

Government documents can be used to (a) acquaint class members with the fact that the U.S. administration is doing some serious work in trying to slow down the arms race; (b) give the class the feeling that there is thus some realism in looking toward the day when the arms race can be halted; (c) remind them of the way that the treasures of God's creation are being consumed by the arms race; (d) give them some sense of excitement about the tremendous strides that could be made in carrying out Christ's command to meet human need (Matt. 25:31-45) if we were freed from the arms race.

Short and easily read government items are: *Sixth Annual Report of the U.S. Arms Control and Disarmament Agency; The Economic and Social Consequences of Disarmament; Comparison of the U.S. and U.S.S.R. Disarmament Proposals; and the Joint U.S./U.S.S.R. Statement of Agreement on Disarmament Principles.*

Progress: The A.C.D.A. report summarizes the activities of that agency in 1966. These include (a) efforts made and progress achieved in negotiating arms control proposals, (b) the kind of research being done to solve the knotty problems that must be worked out to make disarmament possible.

This document is so concise that two class members could summarize the highlights from it in about seven minutes each. One might concentrate on the one or two areas of disarmament negotiation in which the report indicates the most progress is being made. The other person could share with the class some of the interesting types of research on disarmament problems being done by A.C.D.A.

You, as the teacher, might want to lead off with a statement from the short introductory section of the report, describing the activities of A.C.D.A.

Full disarmament: One proposal being negotiated by the A.C.D.A. is for general and complete disarmament (G.C.D.). Both the U.S. and Russia have put forth such plans. The remarkable amount of agreement on major points of these two proposals is shown in the *Joint U.S./ U.S.S.R. Statement.* A class member could present the outline of this item in seven to ten minutes.

If the class wonders why so much agreement has not produced a G.C.D. treaty, the answer can be given them in a few minutes by someone who has read the item comparing the disarmament proposals of the two nations.

Some advance work with a chalkboard could produce a chart that would show the class the similarity between the two sets of proposals, as well as the major differences.

If you have two copies of the comparison items, you might give them to two different members in advance. Ask one to take five minutes in class to speak as though he were the U.S. negotiator explaining why the U.S. believes its G.C.D. plan is more workable. Ask the other member to do the same thing with the Russian proposals.

Peace means prosperity: Many people still believe that disarmament would mean a depression. So it would be important for your class to get the good news on this matter from the pamphlet on the economics of disarming.

One person could read this document in preparation for backing up with facts and figures the answers given by the class to certain questions.

For instance, you might ask, "If world disarmament came, what are some things that could be done with the money that would be saved?" Someone would probably say, "Cut taxes." Your resource person could then report that U.S. experience after World War II and the Korean war shows that significant tax cuts would accompany every meaningful stage of disarmament. Someone else might say, "More housing," or "More recreational facilities," and so on. The chances are that the reader of the pamphlet could point out how disarmament savings could help in those areas.

Perhaps one of the members might feel that the nation is prospering splendidly in the midst of the arms race. He might feel it is difficult to see how we could do any better under disarmament. Again, your resource person would be able to step in with a persuasive paragraph from the document on the economics of disarmament.

Using Audio and Visual Tools

The previous sections contained suggestions for expanding personal awareness and self-expression, and confrontation of the real world through printed materials. Here we offer a glimpse into the world of audio, visual, and audio-visual resources.

The Attitude Scale and the Checklist of Concern are tools for *gathering* information rather than for presenting it. Such devices must usually be created by the group leader for a specific group, and should be based on subject matter related to the resource materials in use by the group.

In addition to the several types of charts treated, a useful one is the PERT chart (Program Evaluation and Review Technique). A group may set a date for the completion of a task (such as a service or action project) and assess the amounts of time required for all steps leading to this completion. Then as time passes and phases are carried out, a group can tell if it is moving fast enough and what parts of the program need special attention.

Some readers may have no difficulty with the medium of

folk music, but have some trouble seeing the relevance to their own concerns of the ideas in this article. Folk music, like other artistic expressions and social commentary, is often produced by persons who are moved by their own painful experiences or their feeling with those who suffer.

With a tool for analysis such as that in the article on secular films, the constant parade of films in commercial theaters becomes a lively resource. Even more accessible are the movies on television, either for personal viewing for later discussion or for group viewing followed by immediate discussion using such a tool.

Tape recording is extremely simple and versatile. The articles on this topic reveal many sources of prepared tapes and ways of making and using your own. Don't forget the possibility of tape-recording a group meeting. This is a valuable technique for evaluating your group members' participation.

One medium not covered in this section is the 8-mm. cartridge film. Availability of commercial 8-mm. films increases by giant steps each year, both in numbers and in fields of interest. Some subject possibilities for homemade 8-mm. films are a tour of a hospital, factory, or slum area; a role play, playreading, or interpretative dance; an interview, a brief talk, or a rapid-fire impressionistic sequence to "blitz the mind open."

A publication of great value in this field is *The Teachers Guide to Media and Methods,* from Media and Methods Institute, Inc., 124 East 40th St., New York, N.Y. 10016.

An Attitude Scale

"Your attitude is showing!" How many times have you been shocked by this statement? What does it mean for an attitude to show?

Underlying our external makeup there is an internal, enduring, and learned predisposition to act a certain way toward an individual or a pattern of thought. This internal framework is the makeup of our attitudes. This largely unconscious "seedbed" determines our way of acting as well as our verbal expression of opinions.

Where do our attitudes come from? The first observation we can make is that attitudes are learned. They are formed as we determine whether we like or dislike the way our needs are met. Many of our attitudes grow out of our relationships with the family. A child tends to learn to react as members of his family do, because in reacting this way he finds himself safely accepted by this important social group.

In all his social relationships a person tends to be like the person who gives him security. Attitudes toward the Bible are developed by this kind of association. If a child grows up in a society that will consider him an atheist or heretic if he questions any portion of the Bible, he likely will attach his salvation to his ability to accept every "jot and tittle" of the Scriptures.

Since attitudes are learned, they may be evaluated and unlearned. But before this can be done, the attitudes must be identified. One way of doing this is through the use of a checklist of attitudes—a scale.

Such a checklist may be made up of a series of statements about a subject. For each statement there should be a multiple-choice answer scaled to show varying reactions. For example: (None, Few, Many) of my daily decisions are influenced by my study of the Bible.

After individuals have marked their reactions, serious

evaluation must follow. Such evaluation of attitudes must be based on some knowledge of attitudes, their meaning, identification, and methods of changing them. A good resource for such a study would be an article on "Attitudes" in one of the more recent encyclopedias. The group probably should mark the checklist before making the study of attitudes. This will avoid putting them on guard, for the study will inevitably cause the group to look seriously at ideas they have previously considered insignificant.

How to go about evaluation presents a problem. If the class has not had many experiences in group work, and if there is a general fear of honesty about oneself in the group, each individual might be asked to write privately on the following or similar questions:

1. How long have I felt this way?
2. What knowledge do I use to support my opinion?
3. How do my closest associates feel about the subject?
4. Can I relate any specific personal needs to my opinion?

Another way of approaching the evaluation would be to use the above questions in small groups of five to eight persons. But they must realize that the groups may not arrive at definite conclusions. The discussion of individual points of the checklist will serve to help individuals see themselves more clearly and also how they have arrived at their conclusions.

To add an additional goal to the discussion, the small groups may be asked to prepare a list of questions they feel need further study by the group. If, for instance, a checklist of attitudes toward the Bible is used, the groups may realize that many attitudes are based on inadequate information. In such a case the groups may formulate goals for further study.

As the groups work, they must constantly be reminded that a person's attitudes are his Achilles' heel. Members studying together should always keep their identity as separate, respected individuals. Growth may stop if sensitive areas are attacked by self-assertive individuals who protect their own attitudes by aggressiveness. Remember that nature has provided all life with the ability to crust over vulnerable areas. Giving a person psychological room to change attitudes will ultimately result in an atmosphere of learning where freedom and activity are the characteristics. Criticism of individuals who do not agree with the other members will result in a group in which aloofness is characteristic.

A sensible group will immediately see that the validity of an attitude does not depend on the number voting for or against. Further learning may tend to support the minority or to prove the truthfulness of the majority view, or it may cast doubt on all members' attitudes and require a painful reeducation.

Checklist of Concerns

In the discussion of the use of an attitude scale or checklist it was evident that verbal opinions concerning a specific subject develop from a person's basic, underlying attitudes.

Opinions may result from inadequate knowledge or be based on a sentiment rather than on reason. On the other hand, they may be based on a thorough study of a field of knowledge. In whatever way our opinions are formed, they are the basis for our concerns.

But not all opinions are held with equal concern. Therefore, the extent of concern felt by a person about an opinion may be rated on a variable scale having at least three general classifications: (1) negative disbelief or no concern; (2) a feeling of uncertainty or intellectual neutrality or intellectual agreement with no emotional attachment; (3) positive intellectual and emotional commitment. Hence, a concern checklist may contain statements like this: "Sending medical and educational missionaries to other countries is helpful. Yes __ No __ Uncertain __"

Factors determining intensity of concern: A number of discernible factors may be used to focus on the extent of a particular concern or set of concerns held by an individual or group:

1. Usually the greater the knowledge used to form an opinion, the greater the concern for that opinion. Consider this opinion: "The United States should open its doors to refugees, whoever they may be." The person who has a knowledge of the needs and suffering of refugees will usually express a higher rate of concern. Those who have no knowledge of the identity of refugees may see nothing to get excited about.

2. However, it should also be noted that as the knowledge level concerning an opinion rises, concern may decrease even to the point of disbelief. As concern decreases, it may raise the extent of concern proportionately for an opposite opinion. Consider this statement: "Most of the really poor people around the world are poor mostly because they are lazy, and they are really happy if agitators do not stir them up." A study of the poor of the world may result in an opposite conclusion. A study of the facts may result in a changed opinion, with a high rate of concern: "Most of the poor people of the world are poor mostly because those of us who are not poor are both consciously and unconsciously keeping them that way."

3. Our concern in regard to an opinion is emotionally charged in direct relationship to our ability to identify, or feel, with the subject. For instance: "I think every person has an equal right to his own views and an equal right to promote these views, whether or not I agree." An individual's concern in this matter may be heightened emotionally if he has had some direct experience of censure of his own views and desires to promote those views. His emotional concern may also heighten for the opposite opinion if he has found himself attacked by freely expressed views.

4. False concerns may be produced by social pressure or by a need for fulfillment regardless of the subject of the opinion. Thus a Negro may vehemently oppose an opinion that "every person has an equal right to good housing, food, job, education." His opposition may be based on his desire to stay alive or to maintain the meager opportunities he already has.

102

Value of the checklist: After rating our concerns in regard to a series of opinions, we may group and evaluate them as an overall life style or pattern. This is possible because a consistent system of attitudes usually underlies our concerns. Thus our opinions and our concern accompanying those opinions seem to follow a consistent pattern. For example, if a series of opinions about international questions is used on the checklist, a quick tabulation can determine an individual's pattern of concern: It may be very narrow, or it may encompass the world.

In the hands of a class leader interested in helping his students know who they are, the extent-of-concern checklist can become a valuable tool. He may use it to help the group set goals for further study. With a checklist filled out by each class member, a committee could use a tabulation as a basis for setting goals. It will tell the committee where the group members presently are in their thinking and commitments.

Another effective use of this kind of instrument would require the checklist to be completed at the beginning of a study and then the same checklist to be filled out at the end. By comparing the two an individual may evaluate his progress or the effect the class study has had on him.

An extent-of-concern checklist may be used to analyze an individual's life stance. It can tell us the kind of person he is at any given point in his life. This analysis may form the basis for future growth. Or it may be used for evaluation of the usefulness of group study. We see its value when we realize that in order to catch a glimpse of who we may become in Christ, we *must* know who we are now.

Charts

Charts are not just interesting diagrams using a set of facts. Rather, a good chart is a visual symbol that uses either graphic and pictorial media or an outline of verbal material to present an orderly and logical relationship between key facts and ideas. The chart's role is to show relationships, such as comparison, relative facts, developments, processes, classification, organization, and proportion.

The creative teacher may find these varied types of visualizations useful:

Tree chart. This "idea picture" is composed of several "roots" that lead into a single "trunk." The branches of the tree represent developments and relationships. Using this visualization to introduce the techniques involved in Bible study would help bring some depth and enlightenment into a study sometimes characterized by an ignorance of source material.

The strong trunk of the tree could carry the label "serious Bible study," while the roots might symbolize the enormous volume of source material. If the trunk and branches are to be healthy and laden with new understandings, the following roots should be used:

commentaries
atlases
Bible dictionaries
modern translations of the Bible

Stream chart. This kind of presentation will show a great variety of elements combined to form one important product. Let's look at some specific areas of biblical study and how a stream chart presentation can guide a group. For instance: If the product we are seeking is knowledge about a specific biblical writer, the chart would show several factors flowing toward the writer. Among them might be the historical and personal circumstances at the time of the writing, the writer's intended audience, his purpose in writing, his choice of literary form, and his central message and characteristic emphases.

We might also seek a similar product in knowledge about the readers a writer had in mind. If so, some of the flowing streams might include a general identification of the readers; their historical and personal circumstances; their language, culture, religious background, and social traits; their characteristic point of view about the writer's subject matter.

Tabular chart. The unique value of this chart lies in its ability to show time relationships. It can be useful in showing the progressive history of a group of people (for instance, the readers mentioned above). It offers a great deal of creative freedom in that pictures may be added to a simple time-line chart, or a series of verbal or pictorial time sequences may be paralleled to show historical relationships of several groups of people.

Flow chart. This pictorial method of presentation will show functional relationships between one idea or group of ideas and another idea or group of ideas. A functional relationship may be shown between a particular passage of Scripture and the resultant ways of acting and living. The chart would show the scriptural passage as the source of the flow. From the source, arrows would show the life concepts resulting from this particular teaching.

Charts and other learning experiences: Charts are of greatest value when used with other methods of the teaching/learning process.

Some charts, such as the tree chart suggested above, will be valuable aids in directing a research committee to the resources needed. Others will give added system to subject matter that is difficult because of its complexity or broad scope. For instance, a series of dramatic presentations of biblical events will come more clearly into focus if they are placed in the perspective of a time line (tabular chart, above).

Perhaps one of the best uses of charts could grow out of the flow chart concept. The chart itself could be the product of group work. Discussion groups could be assigned particular Scripture passages or concepts with the direction to discover some ways they become a part of the life of the Christian. The task of the groups would be to show the *results* of the concept flowing from the assigned Scripture passage or concept. To finish the experience, the whole group could evaluate the charts of the small groups.

Teaching Pictures

Seeing ourselves as others see us is a helpful experience, as Robert Burns observed. Seeing the world as others see it can provide insights into history, our own emotions, or the visions of dreamers. One of the teaching procedures for accomplishing such learning is the use of teaching pictures.

The phrase "teaching pictures" usually applies to those reproductions of paintings or photographs which are printed and distributed along with other curriculum materials. These pictures are chosen for their special relevance to lesson content and distributed for teachers who might not have time to locate appropriate pictures.

Think of the teaching picture as any kind of visualization which aids the learning process. While such a picture might be abstract art, it is more likely to be realistic.

Sources for teaching pictures include the daily newspaper, weekly news magazines, or any other publication that primarily uses pictures rather than words to tell the story.

Teaching pictures can be found also in advertisements, and these are particularly valuable for understanding our system of cultural values, passing fancies and fads, or social patterns. Photographs and flat pictures are two sources of teaching pictures. Photographic slides, filmstrip frames, even movie frames, provide additional resources for teaching pictures.

Whether professionally produced or homemade, teaching pictures aid teaching and learning when they serve a purpose clearly related to the experience. Such purposes include the following: (1) illustrating an experience to which the viewer can relate for action or reaction, (2) evoking an emotion or sentiment, or (3) describing visually a situation or circumstance not experienced by the viewer.

Teaching pictures can be used singly or in groups. If more than one is used during a lesson, decide whether the pictures will be used together or separately. This scheduling influences the method of presentation. If the pictures are to be used as a discussion starter or as a point of departure for a lecture, try mounting all the pictures on a bulletin board. A layout artist can help create interesting arrangements that can supplement the learning experience. On the other hand, if the pictures are to be used at various times during the lesson, stack them on an easel or lay them face down on a table, and show only one picture at a time.

After using the picture, leave it in view of the group while moving on to the next picture. But if this is distracting, turn it over. Always examine the picture display location and viewing sequence in terms of the relationship of the pictures to the total learning experience. Removing a picture from view after it has served its purpose is much better than to risk having it distract the learners' attention during the remainder of the lesson.

Class members could be asked in advance to bring two pictures each to the next session—one *showing* an experience of great personal trust, the other *evoking* a feeling of trustworthiness. When the pictures are presented to the group, let members express what they think or feel about a picture before the person showing it describes what it means to him and why he chose it. Be alert for the varieties of interpretation and reaction to a picture, and center discussion on how we learn to trust by what we experience as well as by what we feel. Never assume a picture communicates to others what it does to you.

The learning situation for using the teaching picture might be other than a regular meeting room. Young adults often go to coffee houses where paintings and sculpture are displayed. Museums, art galleries, and exhibits of photography provide additional locations for viewing and discussing our reactions to visual images.

Although it takes time and effort, a leader might secure a photographer and create a set of slides, prints, or posters for use in a learning situation. While this could be a documentary series, it might be impressionistic, seeking to relate to mood as much as to fact.

When presenting a teaching picture in a learning situation, use language that conveys a willingness to allow each person to react in his own unique way. For example, in showing the picture of a dope addict injecting heroin, ask, "What does this picture say to you?" or "What does this girl know about the search for meaning in life?" After the group responds, relate their answers to the idea of trust or search for meaning.

In understanding the complex world we live in, we need to relate ourselves to the many compartments of living: work, home, recreation, eating, clothes, transportation, and so on. A collection of current advertisements which seek to speak to us in our various areas of concern could help us identify sources of pressure and "answers to meaning" being offered by elements in our society, and could provide a basis for identifying the motivations for our beliefs and actions.

Photographs

A class that intends to enrich its study by using photographs will first need some skill in locating and recognizing superior photographs. Members of a local camera club might be asked to lead a class session on questions like these: What makes a photograph great? What are some of the standard, dependable sources of outstanding photographs—magazines, annuals, books, and so forth?

Many of the best photographs of the year are published in *Photography Annual*.[1] We are here concerned with photographs of similar high quality.

What can photographs do for your study group?

A photograph can be used to open a conversation about a topic that your class tends to avoid, ignore, or forget. It can provide a noncontroversial technique for starting a conversation about a controversial subject. Almost every adult class tends to skip certain topics, such as the ethics of war, interracial marriage, and sex ethics. Some subjects, it is thought, are too "hot" or too embarrassing to touch.

For example, take the cover of *Photography Annual 1965*—a picture of a young woman, blonde, pensive, dressed in an orange bathing suit, standing in shoulder-high, dry grass. This picture can be used to help a class begin talking about the question: What is the Christian's attitude toward his own body? This question must be faced eventually during any study of sexual morality for the Christian.

Mount or display this cover picture so that the class

[1] Ziff-Davis Publishing Co.

can see it comfortably. Begin by asking the class to look at the picture without comment. Then let the class discuss such questions as these, one by one, not rushing too quickly from one to the next: Where is she? What is she thinking? What is she feeling? What is her attitude toward you as you look at her? How does she feel about being a woman? What is her attitude toward her own body?

By the time your class has talked about the photograph in this way, the conversation should be well under way. Questions less directly related to the picture can then be asked: Is bodily existence good or bad, according to Christian faith? How does one's attitude toward his own body relate to sexual morality? The photograph and the class's response to it will assure that the class moves easily into a discussion of questions that might otherwise be embarrassing, controversial, or taboo.

The questions I have listed above follow a sequence. The first is a simple question about the objective content of the picture and requires only a brief, objective answer. The next questions are less objective, more intuitive, more personal. At this point the student can talk about himself while apparently focusing on the picture. The next questions move the conversation away from the picture to the class itself, and its feelings and thoughts about the topic which the photograph has unleashed. The latter can be discussed more easily because of the simple questions about the photograph that started the conversation.

A photograph can be used to make the subject matter of a discussion more concrete, less theoretical. Your class will need to discuss many subjects they may have had only limited personal experience with—the civil rights struggle, war, disarmament, the Roman Catholic Church, poverty, the inner city. Photographs cannot replace firsthand experience, but they are often closer to reality than our second-hand opinions. What your class says and thinks about the morality of war and the need for disarmament can be made more realistic by photographs such as those on pages 52-53 of *Photography Annual 1965*. Photographs like those on pages 184-87 can keep a discussion of the civil rights movement closer to the meaning experienced by men and women immersed in the struggle.

A display of pictures can introduce a unit of study by (1) suggesting in general the subject matter and its scope, (2) showing men and women who are facing the same problems to be faced by the class in studying the unit, (3) arousing interest and curiosity about what is to follow, (4) asking visually some of the questions planned for discussion, (5) summarizing the basic components of the problem to be faced, its origins, present form, and possible solution or outcome.

Photographs can give your class a common experience around which to orient their conversation—a definite focus and a definite starting point. Photographs can define visually the subject matter for any given class session. Constant reference to these photographs can help the class stay on the subject. A display of photographs can be used to preview, outline, or summarize the content of a unit of study.

A display of pictures built by the class as a study develops may serve as a running summary of previous sessions and as a reminder of the real world to which the study has reference.

Folk Music

Many young adults today are very weakly attached to the church. Often they find its authority to be either unconvincing or oppressive. The language of the church—the language of its preaching, its Scriptures, and its liturgy—is seldom their language. The church can speak to young adults effectively only if it constantly tries to build bridges between itself and the world of the young adult. Folk music can be such a bridge.

A class that has never used folk music as a part of its study may wish to begin with a simple, extended, relaxed listening session—perhaps in somebody's home. At this listening session the purpose of the class may be very general. Let the class members listen first of all to become familiar with the words and feeling of the music. Suggest that they listen for ideas they think should matter to the church, for ethical judgments, for concerns that are also Christian concerns. In other words, try to discover in a very general way how the world of the church touches the world of the folk musician.[1]

Folk music and persistent life concerns: Christian education deals with man's persistent life concerns, the questions that occur and recur to every man: Who am I? What is my life all about? What do I mean to others? What do I mean to God? How can I become my best self? What is good? What is bad?

---

[1] At the same time, your class might study the book by William Robert Miller, *The World of Pop Music and Jazz* (St. Louis: Concordia Publishing House, 1965).

These questions are often expressed with greater clarity in the secular culture than within the church. The Christian educator who would speak to such questions may find help by locating the questions within the culture. Where in its art, entertainment, song, and literature is the society asking questions that matter to most or perhaps to all men? Folk music, which is distinguished by its honesty, its elemental humanity, and its directness, is often the place to look.

One good example is a song by Bob Dylan, "Blowin' in the Wind." This folk song is all questions—questions that penetrate the sufferings, anxieties, indifference, and injustice that most men suffer throughout their lives. A song such as this has obvious values for the Christian educator, not because it contains a Christian answer, but because it asks questions that have come from people's lives. If Christians will first listen with respect and learn what men's questions are, they will be better able to declare how their faith speaks to these basic questions.

Folk music and peace: In the concern for peace we find another overlapping of faith, religion, and folk music. One song expressing the horrors of nuclear war is "A Hard Rain's A-Gonna Fall," by Bob Dylan. In some of the most powerful and searing imagery in modern poetry, he describes a world destroyed and poisoned by the "hard rain" of poisonous fallout. It is a world of sad forests, dead oceans, babes threatened by wild animals, men who talk and cannot listen, men who cannot talk, children armed for war.

Another example is Bob Dylan's "Masters of War." You

can find this song in the book *The Freewheelin' Bob Dylan*.[2] This song is directed to the masters of war, by which Bob Dylan means the men who build the guns, the death planes, and the bombs—the men who collect the money and do not suffer.

A Christian hearing this song will have to ask: What feeling does Bob Dylan have about war and about the men he calls the masters of war? Is his reaction to war and to the masters of war Christian? Can this song feed the Christian's mind as he tries to think about the morality of the war industries? What does the church say about the masters of war? How does the church speak to and declare the faith to men whose livelihood comes from building missiles and bombs and weapons? [3]

Folk music and the awakened conscience: One service that folk music can bring to the church is to awaken its conscience. A young adult class might listen to folk music as they ask these questions: Where in folk music is the troubled conscience being expressed? What songs remind me of those problems that should trouble the conscience of the church, the conscience of my class, and my own conscience? Where is the folk singer reminding us of our failure to live in love? Where is he reminding us of injustice, of man's suffering, and of the cracks in human society that prevent fellowship between man and man?

Folk music and love of country: Not all folk music is protest music. There are good folk songs that express in

[2] (New York: M. Witmark and Sons, 1967.)

[3] Outside the field of folk music, you might hear also Benjamin Britten's oratorio *War Requiem* (London—A4255 and OSA1255) as a stimulant to the church's conscience in the face of war.

a simple way a man's love for his country. A class might be interested in examining patriotism as it appears in folk music, in the patriotic hymns in denominational hymnals, in popular songs and, finally, in a recent record called *Day for Decision.*

An example of a folk singer expressing love for country is Pete Seeger's record *God Bless the Grass.* The first song on this album is called "The Power and the Glory"; the last, "My Land Is a Good Land." Each of these is patriotism in the folk idiom. Among popular patriotic songs to be considered are "The Star-Spangled Banner," "God Bless America," "America the Beautiful," and the songs associated with World Wars I and II. Finally, *Day for Decision,* from the field of pop music, is a combination of American militarism, patriotism, and a kind of nationalistic religiosity.

Look at the love for country expressed in these songs. Ask of each song questions like these: What feelings does this singer or writer have about his country? What does he love about it? What about it does he praise and what does he criticize? What does he see as the foundation of his country's greatness? What does he see in his country's future? Do the answers to these questions differ when they refer to the folk song, to the hymn, to the popular patriotic song, and to *Day for Decision?*

Whenever an adult class thinks about patriotism, love of country, or Christian citizenship, the danger of idolizing the nation needs to be a part of its study. Here, also, folk music can be a resource. Consider Bob Dylan's song "With God on Our Side," which tells what one boy learned of his country's history. Dylan says, in effect, that America has claimed in each war to have God on her side and that, in hating the Russians, rearming the Germans, developing chemical warfare, missiles, and nuclear weapons, America still claims to have God on her side.

Dylan may or may not be right; this is not my point in mentioning his song. The point is, he raises the question of idolatry in national life. He calls upon the listener to ask, Has my nation acted as though whatever it does is sanctioned by God? Certainly *some* Americans have felt this way, and this is a danger for all Americans. Just as the nation is not God, so the nation cannot be served blindly. Bob Dylan's song reminds us of this danger and pleads with us to think about it.

Folk music and God's world: A concern for nature comes out in *God Bless the Grass*. This record is composed for the most part of songs about man's misuse of the natural world. Here are songs about the pollution of the Hudson River and the San Francisco Bay, the merciless spread of the cement octopus (the highways), the waste of water, the needless poisoning of animals through the careless use of pesticides.

Conservation, the preservation of natural beauty, and Christian stewardship of God's world are things that matter to the Christian. Adults who think the phrase "Christian stewardship" is dull and rather stilted may find it a living phrase when coupled with the songs of this album, *God Bless the Grass*. The album is a good place to start a study of man and his relationship to nature.

Folk songs and a world view: The Christian faith is a way of looking at life, a perspective on life as a whole.

117

In other words, the Christian faith is a world view. The Christian faith can be understood best if it is contrasted with other world views. Often a folk song will suggest a way of looking at life as a whole or of making an evaluation of the world.

One example is Dylan's "Desolation Row" on the record *Highway 61 Revisited*. "Desolation Row" is, in my judgment, a phrase that describes the world to Dylan, at least in this song. Listen to it. Get Dylan's feeling about the world and the life around him, about its ugliness, its beauty, its values, and its betrayals. Compare this with the world view of the Christian faith, what our faith declares to be good and bad, just and unjust, lovely and unlovely.

A class can use music to see better what some of the possible world views are. Comparing "Desolation Row" and "This Is My Father's World" would allow a Christian to know better what he actually thinks about the world. Which of these songs comes closest to describing the world he sees and lives in and reacts to? Many times Christians respond more strongly than they realize to world views that are only half Christian or non-Christian.

A folk song, then, can help your adult class by introducing into it ideas, feelings, and perspectives that your class can share or respond to but would ordinarily fail to discuss.

Secular Films

An adult group can experiment quite fruitfully with the use of secular films as resources in Christian education.

Certainly not all films are valuable for this purpose, and none of them are valuable if your group has no method of unlocking their relevance.

G. William Jones, author of *Sunday Night at the Movies*[1] told in an earlier magazine article why some secular films can be of value to the church. He discounts the value to the church of the "extravaganzas" and "colossal spectaculars." He continues:

But Hollywood is also producing the "intimate" film which is inward and personal. These films move toward deeper examination of the wondrous enigma of man and his relationships with other men, with his word, and with his own self. Such films have integrity, for they are concerned with authenticity, with portraying life "as it is." The intimate film follows the individual with an unswerving eye into the most private recesses of his thoughts, habits, and decisions. Psychological motivations are as important—or more—than outward action.

Such a film is almost sure to make us uneasy, because to see another person exposed is to see at least something of ourselves also exposed.[2]

In life, as opposed to fantasy, personalities, motivations, and moral issues are never clean and simple; they are cluttered, complex, and problematic. A secular film is of value to the church when it is willing to be as complex as life. *The Pawnbroker* is such a film, as are also, to name a very few, *Who's Afraid of Virginia Woolf? The Hustler,*

---

[1] (Richmond: John Knox Press, 1967.)

[2] "The Church and Secular Films," in *Christian Advocate*, June 18, 1964, p. 7. Copyright © 1964, by The Methodist Publishing House.

8½, Juliet of the Spirits, Zorba the Greek, and *The Three Faces of Eve.*

Jones says these films can help the church see *"where* the traditional symbols of the faith (sin, grace, death, forgiveness, resurrection) come alive in the common occurrences of everyday life." How can the Christian person move beyond a knowledge of *sin, grace,* and *forgiveness,* as words, to a conscious experience of the realities themselves? How can the Christian identify *sin, grace, death, forgiveness,* and *resurrection* when he meets them in daily life? One way is to see that Christian education deals with realities instead of words only. At just this point secular films may become valuable in Christian education.

They will be valuable, however *only* if a method of unlocking them is available. Jones proposes the following for use in a discussion of any secular film:

I. Questions to help participants remember *all* of the film and not just the last part or the climactic parts:

    1. Which scene do you recall most vividly?

    2. Which inanimate objects do you recall?

    3. Which music?

    4. Which minor character do you remember strongly?

    5. Which room or setting?

    6. Which love scene?

    7. Where were you conscious of sounds?

(By the time these questions have circuited the entire group a few times, almost the entire picture has been brought up and almost everyone has been eager to participate—the whole film is now "present" to the minds of those in the discussion group.)

II. Questions that help the people to clarify their subjective reactions to the characters and situations.

1. Do you recall your own moods while watching?
2. Do you recall any moments when you or the group laughed nervously?
3. To which character were you drawn, at what time in the film? Did you change your viewpoint?
4. By what character were you repelled, at what time in the film? Did you change?
5. Were you ever angry with any of the characters? Why?
6. Did you ever feel uneasy with any of them? When?

III. Questions that bring to bear the language-symbols traditional to the Christian faith—but now in a life-interpretive way:

1. Where was "sin" occurring in this film?
2. Where did you see "grace" in this film?
3. Did you see any "divine activity" going on?
4. Where did you see the "Christ-event" in the film—that is where did you see someone presented with an opportunity for realizing the "saving truth" about who he really is, for finding a new relationship with himself and others?
5. Where did you see "death and resurrection" in the film—that is, where did you see a dying of an old, inauthentic way of living and an emergence into a new way of life—from "brokenness to wholeness"?
6. Through whom did Christ seem to speak to others? [3]

[3] *Ibid.* p. 8.

Tape Recordings

This discussion of the use of a tape recordings comes from a teacher of a young adult class:

My young adult class is studying "Affluence and Poverty: Dilemma for Christians." Recently I was set to thinking by a radio program. Michael Harrington was talking about poverty and how it relates to other social problems. At first the name Harrington didn't register with me, but later in the program I realized that Harrington is an adviser to the government in its antipoverty program. All the way through this program I kept thinking, "If only this were broadcast on Sunday morning instead of Thursday night. If my class could listen to Harrington discuss poverty, our whole study of affluence and poverty would benefit. Too bad, I thought, but this is Thursday, not Sunday, and this program will end at nine o'clock."

Then I learned something that opened all kinds of new doors. At the end of the program, the announcer said, "The program you have just heard is available as a tape recording from the Center for the Study of Democratic Institutions. . . ." I thought to myself, "That will bear investigation. I wonder how many other programs there are on prerecorded tapes that would be useful to my young adult class?"

After I wrote the Center for the Study of Democratic Institutions (Box 4068, Santa Barbara, California 93103), they sent me a catalogue titled *Tapes.* On one tape Newton Minow talks about ways of improving the quality, variety, and coverage of television. On another, Elmo Roper asks,

"What can the individual American do about democracy?" On still another, Ralph Greenson, psychiatrist, talks about the perils of loving and about the rarity of intense friendships in our time.

I realized soon that many of these tapes tie in directly with units our class will study. For example, "A Walk on the West Side" (No. 69 in the catalogue) ties in closely to "Affluence and Poverty"; and "The Warless World" (No. 10) ties in to "Disarmament." There are tapes on race, on peace and war, on the world around us, on challenges to democracy, on capitalism, socialism, and communism, on technology and men, on the Supreme Court and the Constitution, and on America and Americans.

The Department of State has a library of circulating audio tapes. For example, they have a basic series on the conduct of foreign policy. The first of these is a discussion of the purpose and work of the Foreign Service. I am already planning to use it to supplement the unit "Invest Your Life." My first letter of inquiry went to Tapes Officer, Office of Media Services, Room 4831, Department of State, Washington, D.C. 20520. These State Department tapes are available for loan without charge. The tape called "Considerations Behind a Nuclear Nonproliferation Treaty" will be useful when we study disarmament.

One more lead to prerecorded tapes came to me in the form of a catalogue from the Reigner Recording Library. The scope of this library is suggested by the index to the catalogue, which lists over seventeen hundred men and women who are heard or seen on the recordings and films in the Reigner collections. W. H. Auden, James Baldwin, Lincoln Barnett, James Conant, Henry Fonda, William

Faulkner, and Paul Tillich are a few of the names that excite me. For example, Tillich's famous lectures on "Love, Power, and Justice" are available on a set of seven tapes.

Reigner has recordings of sermons, worship services, evangelistic crusades, theological lectures, and religious radio programs, as well as tapes on mental health, music, and drama. I got my catalogue by writing Reigner Recording Library, Audio-Visual Center, Union Theological Seminary, Richmond, Virginia 23227.

When I first suggested to my class that we use a tape recorder occasionally, three members said they owned one. Another member suggested that we be more inventive than I had been. He thinks that using prerecorded tapes is just about the most uncreative use of a tape recorder. We brainstormed the question, What are some ways our class might use a tape recorder? Here is a list we made:

1. Record interviews with resource people who cannot attend a class session.

2. Record a class discussion and play it back for evaluation.

3. Record material from radio and television that is appropriate to supplement a unit of study.

4. Build a collection of tapes for the church library.

5. Record observations as your class takes a field trip.

6. After each class session, record immediately a summary of that session for replay as review at the beginning of the next session. Do this throughout the unit, and use all the summaries together to review the entire unit during the concluding session.

7. Share your class sessions with hospitalized or disabled members of your class.

8. Spark interest in a new study by introducing it to your class in this way: Record a selection of key questions from the study, or a selection of key quotations from famous men on the topic of the study, or a selection of key Scriptures on the topic. Play your tape as an introduction to the unit.

9. If there are hymns that bear on the topic your class is studying, ask your church choir to tape several of these for use in your class.

10. If you are studying a topic like "The Church's Role in Social Change," conduct and record ten three-minute interviews with key laymen in your church to get a sampling of opinion against which to view the opinions of your own class or the opinions of the writer of the unit.

11. If your class is concentrating on a particular biblical passage, ask three or four persons who are skilled in oral interpretation and reading to record the passage. As your class listens to the three readings, shades and varieties of meanings will be heard in the passage that silent reading and discussion might not reveal.[1]

A Tape-Recorded Panel Discussion

Everyone can benefit from having additional viewpoints brought to his attention. One way to do this is to interject

[1] You may pursue further the usefulness of the tape recorder by reading *The Tape Recorder*, by Robert Sloan, Jr. (Visual Instruction Bureau, University of Texas, Drawer W, University Station, Austin, Texas 78712).

into a group the thinking of other persons by using a tape recording of a discussion that took place at another time and place.

Focus your attention on the purpose for having additional viewpoints brought to your learning experience, not on the technical problems. What will be accomplished by having the opinions of additional persons in your learning situation? Are you seeking a wider age span, different political views, more facts and experience, specialized information not generally available, or involvement of persons who otherwise could not be present?

Another contribution of a tape-recorded panel discussion is its bringing to the learning situation examples of types of people who might be encountered in various ways. It might not be possible to have high school dropouts speak to your group face-to-face, but they might be willing to tape-record an informal conversation that would be similar to a panel discussion.

Opportunities for recording discussions are especially plentiful since it is not always necessary to have the participants sitting down in a formal setting. Indeed, not all the participants have to be physically present at the same time and place, although this is usually desirable. Sometimes it is possible to tape-record a series of talks by different persons over a period of time, and then edit them so as to form a panel discussion.

Editing is not an easy process technically or morally. When taking responsibility to remove something another person has said from his comments or to change the context by interspersing the comments of others, be sure that basic ideas are not changed, that limiting qualifications are not omitted, and that important statements are not deleted. Likewise be certain that those who edit the tape recording know exactly how, when, and where the original comments were recorded, why the editing was done, and that they remember the limitations that editing imposes upon content. Such understanding must not be assumed, since many people are unaware of the technical possibilities of tape-recording techniques.

Choosing persons to participate in a tape-recorded panel discussion usually requires careful planning. Are they the most representative of a particular group? Do they speak from genuine experience, research, or a combination of both? Are they sufficiently skillful in the use of language that they can convey meaning by using only words?

Most important, does the prospective panel member have anything significant to say which has not been heard before or is not generally known by the intended audience? That is, will the discussion be worth the time and effort of recording it in the first place, and will it be equally worth the time and effort of those who will listen to it? A leader must be sure he answers these two questions honestly and accurately if this learning procedure is to have any genuine value.

Remember that the average listening span of persons is less than five minutes, and thereafter the mind is likely to be distracted or wander; and for younger persons the listening span is considerably less. Obviously the tape-recorded panel discussion must be concise if it is to be effective as a learning procedure.

Listening attention can be guided and increased if people know what they are listening for. Outline, preferably on a chalkboard or wall chart, the purpose of the discussion, the purpose for listening, a description of the original recording situation, and the names, titles, and reasons for having the participants; reference can be made to this information during the listening experience. More important, let the group prepare itself by listing questions in a similar manner. Include a final question like, Was anything unexpected said?

A few simple procedures will make the presentation of a tape-recorded panel discussion an effective learning experience. First, be sure everyone can hear clearly. This refers not only to the volume of the recording playback, but to the quality of the tape recording. If possible, test play the recording, and remember that people in a room soak up an enormous amount of sound.

Second, place the speaker so that everyone in the group has a line of sight directly to the speaker. This means set the speaker high, at ear level rather than at waist level.

Third, keep the presentation as brief as possible. Consider the possibility of stopping the playback at appropriate places to see what answers to questions have been found thus far.

Fourth, consider using pictures, slides, or filmstrips to accompany the tape recording when this will aid learning by illustrating events, situations, people, or objects. Each item should be used only because it contributes to the learning from the panel discussion. Care should be taken not to create a distraction.

Taped or Filmed Radio or Television Shows

Our world seems to be living in an eternal Gethsemane. We cannot avoid feeling this when we live in the confines of personal and group relationships such as would exist in an elevator that seemed to rise endlessly, always taking on more passengers with no destination. Sometimes the hellish heat of such a situation is felt in the terror of war or tension between large groups of people as they feel the aimlessness of a world that both shrinks and swells. Sometimes it is felt in the loneliness of a racial demonstration involving persons who feel the frustration of a world that both runs at them and runs away from them.

Sometimes the heat develops in the life of a shaggy-headed, despairing teen-ager who listens to the stereophonic world as one speaker shouts, "Grow up, be adults," and the other says, "Remember, you are youth. Don't touch the adult world." This kind of paradoxical world view inevitably created by "just livin' " produces a life image that is both quite inhuman and vividly human.

Christian education must realize that it has no choice in whether the world will be in its classroooms or not. Indeed, the world is there when people who make the news or those who watch or listen to newscasts are present. Christian education must help students of the gospel find the meaning and truth in the midst of all this.

Taped television and radio programs: Some groups have found that taped radio and television newscasts and other programs are of real value in helping individuals deal with world events.

Using a tape recorder to record radio and television newscasts is an easy matter. It is not necessary to see the pictures on a television newscast in order to know the content of the program.

For instance, a class may decide to try to come to grips with the issue of war and the Christian gospel. A series of recorded news programs could raise the issues very well. After hearing some of these programs, one or two persons could present some background on the Christian attitude toward war, historically and biblically. For this subject the speakers would find Roland H. Bainton's book, *Christian Attitudes Toward War and Peace,* or *A Theological Word Book of the Bible,* edited by Alan Richardson, to be helpful resources.

A reaction panel of three or four people might prepare themselves to discuss the question: How should we Christians respond to the Vietnam conflict? A next step might be for the entire class to be divided into small groups of five to eight to react to the panel. When an issue as emotionally charged as this one comes to the entire group, strong, prepared leadership is a must.

Recorded radio or television programs are not limited to the subject of war. There are numerous possibilities—for example, youth culture, legislative issues, changing moral standards, race problems, international relations. Care should be taken that the class receives enough basic information to come to some studied conclusions. An opinion-giving session is of little use unless impartial, accurate material has been presented.

Programs on 16mm film: Many provocative television

programs are now being made available on 16mm film. Most of the programs from Columbia Broadcasting System's "Look Up and Live" series have been produced on film. Other such films available include *The Detached Americans,* which discusses social apathy, and *A Time for Burning,* whose subject is race and the local congregation. The list lengthens every day and is now providing us with some of the best material available on contemporary subjects.

How can these films best be used? A small work group from the class should preview the film, making sure that the subject matter adequately speaks to the goals of the class. This group should then plan the use of the film in class. (See pages 118-21.)

One possibility would be to divide the class into listening groups prior to viewing the film. Each listening group should be given a definite question or item to look for. After viewing the film, the listening groups should have an opportunity to discuss it in terms of their listening task. A report to the total class from the listening groups should be followed by an opportunity for individual reactions within the total group.

Another possibility would be to include a presentation by a panel prior to the viewing of the film. The panel should be prepared to give some background to the subject matter of the film as well as a clear summary of materials within the church that might speak to the subject; this would include biblical and theological materials. The viewing of the film could be followed by small discussion groups who would deal with the content of the film in terms of the material presented by the panel.

Procedures for Group Involvement

Some teachers of adults mistakenly assume that they must either lecture or lead discussion. They feel that if they deliver a prepared presentation with no feedback, they can keep control of the situation, avoid conflict, be sure of what will be said, and come to a neat conclusion. They may feel that the only alternative to the lecture is a general discussion, which may get out of hand in uncontrolled hostility, or degenerate into a pooling of ignorance.

The procedures in this section, possibly used together with others, are designed to provide for involvement that is deeper than merely listening. But by focusing a group's attention and participation, they prevent the group from falling easily into argument and aggressiveness. A prime consideration is to see that persons are involved with subject matter and experience, instead of giving superficial opinions based on no information.

A Speaker with Listening Groups

Suppose your class has chosen a rather broad topic as the theme for their study. Suppose, also, that they wish to have a speaker for a certain session. What procedure can the group use for making this an effective, worthwhile session?

First, the speaker will need guidance so he can focus his presentation on the interests of the group. Prior to inviting the speaker, the class should attempt to discover what the main interests of their members are in this particular field. To do this, they could be organized into small groups and asked to take five to ten minutes to choose some specific problems they would like the speaker to discuss. At the end of this activity, the recorder-reporter of each group should report either to the total class or to the teacher. This information will be helpful in selecting the speaker and will also give the speaker some guidance.

The following suggestions are given with the supposition that the general topic is "A Christian Standard of Success" and that the class has indicated a great interest in the matter of how to succeed in becoming a whole person. On the basis of this decision, the class would seek a speaker whose primary interest and experience relates to the development of human personality and the interaction of human beings. Such a speaker might be found in the person of a minister, a school counselor, a social psychologist, or an industrial relations counselor.

Organizing: As with many general topics, the group will find it fruitful to organize the listening by setting up listening groups. If the class is small, each listening group could consist of just one or two persons. Preferably, the listening groups would contain four to six and not more than eight persons. This seems to be the best size for securing participation in discussion by all or most of the group members.

Planning: Ideally, a planning committee of the class will have worked out the subtopics assigned to the listening groups. If there is no permanent committee for developing and structuring the class sessions, a temporary committee could be set up. If the small-group device was used to narrow the subject to make it more manageable, the reporters from the groups could make up the temporary planning committee.

This committee of reporters, using the notes from their groups, could quickly work out a list of questions and problems that seemed to interest the class members most in relationship to achieving success in becoming a whole person. The group reporters could probably develop such a list in ten or fifteen minutes.

Listening: Each listening group is asked to listen for a particular idea or for insights on a certain problem or for material helpful in answering a specific question.

With a speaker who is developing the subject of how to achieve success in becoming a whole person, the listening groups might be assigned to listen for ideas relating to such subtopics as these:

How do we define success in the matter of becoming a whole person?

How do we improve our self-image and self-confidence?

How can we develop more positive attitudes in our work?

134

How can we develop better relationships with other people in general?

How can we develop better relationships with members of the opposite sex in particular?

Discussion: After the speech is finished, each listening group can form a small circle and discuss the emphasis assigned to it for listening.

In some cases, there will be widely differing interpretations within the group as to what the speaker actually said or intended to say on a particular point. This is to be expected, as each of us interprets what we hear from the background of experience and attitudes that we bring to it. What one member of the group feels was an encouragement to self-centeredness could be heard by another as a desirable emphasis on self-improvement. What one describes as encouragement to be pushy at work, another will view as praiseworthy suggestions on how to exercise initiative on the job.

The use of listening groups ensures that more thoughtful attention will be given to the speaker's information and insights, that important points will less likely be overlooked, and that class members will be more actively involved.

Questions

Questions are one of the basic tools in the teacher's kit. Paul Vieth, in his book *How to Teach in the Church*

School, included a chapter titled "How to Ask Questions."
He asked these questions at the beginning of his chapter:
"Why should a teacher ask questions? Is it good practice to
plan in advance the questions to be asked in a class session?
If questions can be made of value in teaching, are there
any principles which might help a teacher to ask questions
well?" [1]

Questions can be used in many wrong ways in teaching.
Some questions are not truly questions. Teachers frequently ask questions for their own benefit, not for the
benefit of the group. Their questions are motivated by
their own personal needs and inadequacies.

Occasionally questions are assertions in disguise. For
example, think of the question asked by Pilate, "What is
truth?" This is obviously an assertion that there is no truth.
It tells us that Pilate was cynical about truth. Many questions that we hear in adult classes are statements in disguise.
Teachers or class members may be more concerned to state
their own position than to draw out thoughts of other class
members. But because they have a superficial commitment
to discussion and free exchange of ideas, they frame their
assertions in the form of questions.

*At other times questions are used to avoid taking a posi-
tion of any kind.* Some teachers and class members always
respond to a question with a counter question. They avoid
taking a position in this way and still maintain the appear-
ance of loyalty to the exchange of ideas. As a matter of fact,
with their counter questions they are sidestepping any

[1] (Philadelphia: The Westminster Press, 1935), p. 132.

exchange of ideas. A counter question may not be a true question at all.

Questions are also misused if they are asked primarily to benefit the teacher rather than the class. Questions used in this fashion may be simply tools for expressing the self-will of a teacher who has decided in advance what the class ought to talk about. After having decided this, he may by his questions carefully guide their conversation to *his* goals. Obviously, under these conditions no real interaction between the members of the class can take place.

Some teachers ask questions that do not provoke thought but that call for the parroting of simple one- or two-word answers. These questions are answered by filling blanks. For example, the teacher who feels some compulsion to ask a question but who really wants to lecture, may ask a question like one of these: "John Wesley was born in —————?" Or, His brother was —————?" Or, "He preached in the open fields at —————?" This kind of question is not meant to encourage discussion. It is meant to give the teacher the feeling that he has given the class a chance to talk. But he has really never stopped talking.

A question can be a very aggressive instrument in the hands of a teacher or student who likes to tear people down. Questions may express hostility as well as desire to learn. An aggressive person can literally tear into someone with questions that intend to perplex, trap, embarrass, or stump him. A question may be a form of attack. Again, this is not a true question at all.

A particular conviction about adult students is basic to using questions well. A teacher who believes that the adult student brings to the class experience worth sharing will try to frame questions that will help that experience become the property of the whole class. The adult learns by sharing his experience with others. An adult class is most effective when the sharing of experience takes place often, easily, and without hesitation. A teacher who wants to be a catalyst will use questions that make the exchange of ideas easy.

So far, these ideas about questions have been rather negative. Following are some ways in which questions can help adults learn.

The most obvious and simple use of a question is to gain information. However, even this can be misused if the teacher supposes that all the information is in only a few minds. Other class members may come to look habitually to these people for all the answers. If the maximum learning comes from the widest participation, questions should ordinarily be directed toward the entire class.

Questions may be used to help class members think. Questions may provoke thought, assist thought, and on occasion force thought. Or they may draw out of a person a more complete statement of an idea he has expressed poorly or partially. They may be used to see that the ideas are clarified. Occasionally a class member will state an idea poorly. Vague ideas are not helpful for sharing experience. A teacher may use questions to guide a class member as he tries to make his ideas precise and clear. An idea is not clear until the language is unambiguous, and it is stated in words that can be understood by other members of the class. Ordinarily it should be stated in more than one way, using more than one vocabulary. When an idea has been developed and related to contrasting ideas, it has been stated clearly enough to become part of a learning experience.

Questions can be used to keep a class discussion moving. Sometimes a class in the middle of a discussion will turn to the teacher, expecting him to resolve the problem at hand. Class members may be unable to live with the tension of unresolved questions. They may throw questions at the teacher that, if answered, would do one of two things: They would stop the discussion, or they would cast the teacher in the role of an expert. When questions are asked that have either of these effects, a teacher may legitimately respond with a counter question. A counter question at a time like this would throw back on the class the responsibility of thinking and would make plain to the class that the teacher is not to be used as an escape from thought.

What are some techniques that go into using questions well? The first may require patience. *A teacher must be willing to wait.* Questions will not always be answered instantly. Sometimes they will not be answered at all. But a teacher who is afraid of silence, who fidgets while waiting for an answer, or who wants to give an answer of his own will not use questions effectively. If the question is provocative, the student will have to think before he answers. Courtesy, if not teaching skill, would suggest waiting. More often than not, it is better to leave a question unanswered than to force premature and thoughtless answers or to hand out canned answers each time. The simple act of waiting will do more to gain a response than almost anything else.

Why do some teachers have difficulty waiting for the class's response? Fear, embarrassment, and their own insecurity are often the cause. A teacher may fear that his question is not understood. When he must wait, this fear may grow. It may grow so strong that he is guided or controlled, not by the needs of the class, but by his own fears. He may then shut off the silent thinking that his class is doing in order to allay his own fears. A skilled teacher will let the question do its work at a pace determined by the students and not by his own need to be reassured.

A teacher may refuse to wait because he believes that the answer he has to give is really better than any answer he may expect from the class. His lack of confidence in the class may lead him to give his own answer to his own question so quickly that the question becomes rhetorical.

A teacher may refuse to wait for fear of conflict. He may ask a question and see immediately from the reactions of the class that controversy will result. A sudden fear of controversy may cause him to do an about-face and answer his own question as quickly as possible.

A teacher may refuse to wait because he has preconceived ideas about how the class will respond. "Those dumb people will never speak up." A class may have a long history of silence and refusal to participate. A teacher may know this and assume that waiting for a response is a waste of time. But this can become a vicious circle because the class will learn that the teacher, even if he goes through the motions of asking a question, does not expect a response. So the teacher and the class play the game of trying to start a discussion without expecting, on either side, that any kind of discussion will happen.

Many a question has been allowed to die because it had only one form. If a teacher asks a question once and no response is forthcoming, this may say something about his ability to phrase a question. It may say very little about the class's ability to deal with that question. Only after such a question has been stated in more than one way has a class been given a fair chance to react.

Should a teacher prepare a list of questions in advance of the class session? The answer to this is almost *yes and no. Yes,* because it can help; *no,* because some dangers go along with this practice. A list of questions may be prepared in advance if the teacher does not fall in love with his list and let it become something that must be used from beginning to end. If the first question on his list can set off an entire hour of creative discussion, then the rest of the list becomes a danger to the class and a temptation to the teacher.

Framing questions in advance can help the teacher practice stating questions in a way that is direct, simple, and appropriate. But these questions should not become commitments. The way a question is phrased after the class begins, the time allowed for that question, and the pertinence of the question to a given session must all be a part of the teacher's response to what happens once the class session has begun.

In *How to Teach in the Church School* Paul Vieth lists these among the characteristics of a good question.

A good question deals with matters that are important in the development of the session.

A good question asks one thing and asks it clearly and definitely.

A good question, if it is intended to do more than merely secure an item of information, is one which provokes thought.

141

The question should be within the knowledge and experience of the pupil, just like every other part of the lesson.

A good question should not require the teacher to give hints as to the answer or to "pump" for the right answer.[2]

A Symposium

The more common form of the symposium requires several speakers. Each speaker is expected to develop some particular part of the subject. The purpose of the symposium is to bring the class a wider range of information and viewpoints than is possible when only one speaker is heard. Also class attention is more easily held by the change of pace which several speakers provide.

An example: When the subject is a general one with which we have had a great deal of experience, such as *freedom and authority,* symposium members can come from within the class. The leader might select several class members and meet with them in advance to work out the most natural division of the subject; for example, What are the nature, the necessity, the limits of freedom? of authority?

The chairman needs to be ready with questions that will help symposium members explore the tension between

[2] *Ibid.,* pp. 136-37.

freedom and authority: Can there be growth without freedom to challenge authority? Can there be stability without the authority to set limits to freedom? When does freedom become irresponsibility? When does authority become tyranny?

Symposium members might use events from the American Revolution to illustrate the tension between freedom and authority. The colonists who disguised themselves as Indians and boarded British ships to throw British tea into the Boston harbor were acting in protest against tax laws they thought to be unjust. Americans today regard those early colonists as heroes striking a blow for freedom against laws that served the interest of the controlling group rather than the interests of the colonists. How did those in authority regard the act? As a deed of responsible freedom? Or as one of irresponsible destructiveness?

The symposium might want to help class members see how difficult it is for people to be objective in redefining the meaning of freedom and authority in relationship to the problems of their age.

The dominant economic, social, and racial groups in any society make and enforce the rules in that society. Can any dominant group ever be impartial and objective about the actions of those who feel the laws are unjust and who thus feel compelled to act in defiance of them? How did the Pharaoh react to the Hebrews' request for freedom from harsh working conditions? (Exod. 5.) How did the Pharisees respond when Jesus acted to set man free from crippling religious legalisms? (Mark 2:23 through 3:6.)

The symposium can encourage class members to decide whether these experiences in our religious and political past have anything to say to us about situations today where legal and political authority is being challenged by minority groups. How do the various forms of protest used in the past compare with the actions today of those who seek increased freedom in the form of open housing, equal opportunity in employment and education, and the right to vote without any coercion or intimidation?

Groups create a symposium: For another type of symposium divide the whole class into groups. Let these groups discuss one or two key points or questions relating to the topic of the day. The group leaders can then constitute a symposium, with each presenting his group's conclusions. Time should be left for the class to discuss the opinions and findings presented by the symposium speakers.

When the topic has one or more key points on which widely differing conclusions can be reached, it might be best to have all the subgroups discuss one particular point. After the presentations, the chairman might let the speakers become a panel and discuss the differences of opinion that exist among them. It is the chairman's task to select the more important points of disagreement and to see that no symposium member dominates or bullies the others.

The chairman is also responsible for helping the symposium participants make the discussion a genuine exploration rather than a round of verbal attacks. A little time spent with the participants before the session in formulating the ground rules will make the session richer for the class and easier on the chairman.

A Panel Discussion

When to use a panel: The subject matter must be right. For instance, suppose the class has run across Rudolf Bultmann's idea of demythologizing the New Testament, and no one, including the teacher, has ever heard of this concept before. This would *not* be the time to organize a panel. A much more helpful procedure would be to invite a resource person for a session or two. Then, after each person in the class has had a chance to do some reading, the time might be right to set up a panel to discuss "The Implications of Bultmann's Theory for Modern Bible Interpretation."

How to select the members: First, do not ask a member of the class during the session. If he is a shy person he may say *yes,* but then not follow through. Persons asked hastily may say *yes* without giving a thought to the amount of time for preparation. It is all right to ask for volunteers during the session after giving them a few moments to think it over. But the best procedure is to ask persons privately so that the purpose of the panel presentation can be explained.

Second, try to get persons to serve on a panel who have different points of view on the subpect, or at least ask persons to represent different points of view. This suggestion is not made to open the way for a heated argument. Rather, persons with different points of view can expose the subject under discussion so that the whole range of ideas related to it can be considered by the class members.

For a panel to be successful, the area of the discussion

should be defined so that it can be handled in the time allotted to it. The subject should be introduced in such a way that each member knows where it fits in relation to the goals of the study. Each panel member should have been given hints as to where he can find resource material if he needs it. A moderator should be selected to see that the discussion is kept on the track. Always reserve time for the other class members to ask questions of the panel members as well as of one another.

How many persons? The number should vary with the situation, of course. Conditions that would determine the number of panel members for a given situation would include the nature of the subject to be discussed, the amount of time available for the class session, and the number of people in the class.

If the subject matter is complicated, it might require a detailed introduction. In this case, a panel of two members might be enough. Each could make a ten-minute opening statement from opposite points of view and then discuss between them the points of their presentations before inviting the class members to ask questions or give their opinions. On the other hand, if the material is familiar and persons already have opinions, four or five panel members, with one serving as moderator, could exchange ideas freely right from the start.

The more limited the time for a panel discussion, the more limited the number selected for the panel. If too many persons are selected, each one may have time to make only one contribution; or perhaps there will not be enough time available to generate a flow of ideas. Such a situation should be avoided. This points up to the importance of careful planning for a panel discussion.

Another factor in determining the number of persons for a panel would be the number of persons in the class. Perhaps this is too obvious to mention, but some teachers may think that a panel cannot be used because the class is small. It is conceivable that even in a class of five a two-man panel could be set up. On the other hand, if a class is very large the frequent use of panels might prevent some members from becoming involved. In this case, breaking the class into small groups for discussion and having each group choose a member to represent it on a summary panel discussion involving the whole class works well and gives everyone a chance to participate.

Why use a panel? A panel is a good educational tool when properly organized and used at the right place, because it involves the class members in the learning transaction. It gives panel members and class members alike the chance to relate to given ideas from their own experience of life, using their own words to define and explore the ideas. Thus, through involvement of class members in the learning experience, an atmosphere is created in which insight is most likely to take place.

Further, a panel discussion helps certain people open up because it gives them the "right" to participate. Many adults are still suffering from the wounds of a strict or highly structured educational experience in their early years. It is difficult for them to enter freely into debate. Being designated a panel member gives a class member the right to speak. Also, in panel discussion people in a class get involved with one another's existence. They open up. They get to know one another and hopefully, get to the point of more readily accepting one another. This is the groundwork for the creation of the redemptive relationship and the working of the Holy Spirit.

A Reactant Panel

Reactant panels can be very valuable in helping speakers communicate with an adult class. Such a panel consists of two or three members of the class, usually selected by the teacher. The panel members direct questions to the speaker for purposes of clarification and elaboration.

Suppose the subject is the enlargement of national freedom through the establishment of a limited world federation with sufficient power to end war and the arms race. A reactant panel, composed of class members with differing points of view, can keep the speaker from passing too easily over some of the problems involved. They can also help bring out some benefits that may appeal to special interests in the class.

If the speaker is agreeable to the idea, panel members might even interrupt the speaker with questions about points that need to be clarified if the audience is not to be confused. Some speakers, though, may prefer not to be interrupted. In any case, the primary role of the reactant panel comes at the end of the speech in helping to clarify the subject the speaker dealt with.

Perhaps the subject of freedom and authority is to be approached by having someone speak to the class on the question, How much democracy is really possible in a society as large and complex as ours? A teacher of social problems, political science, or modern history might be an appropriate person to fill such an assignment.

Warming up: It would be helpful to the reactant panel members to meet with the speaker for thirty minutes prior to the session. The speaker could give the reactors a five-minute summary of his speech and then discuss it with them for the remaining twenty-five minutes. As a result, the speaker could relate his material more closely to the interests of the class. The reactors will be better able to ask relevant questions.

For example, the speaker may be making the point that political freedom requires participation in the democratic processes of government. "Failure to participate," says the speaker, "allows power to be gathered up in the hands of the few that do take part." Without a reactant panel, this could be just another Fourth-of-July statement that pleases the ear without enlightening the mind. Since the reactant panel had a preclass session with the speaker, they are prepared for such phrases and can follow the speech with questions that assist the speaker in transforming such oratory into the hard realities of existing political life.

"Sure, God made us to be free, and we should therefore try to strengthen freedom by taking part in the political process," states a reactant. "But, how can we really do this when we don't know any men in the state or national offices, when the issues are so complex and vast, and when everything is in such a rapid state of change? How can we even vote intelligently, let alone do anything more significan than voting?"

Raising tough questions: The reactant panel can then raise the tough questions that the other class members might not raise because it would not seem "polite." One such question might be: Which is more important to the party when it is selecting a candidate, high principles or high voter appeal?

The panel can also raise issues the speaker may hold back because he feels it might not be courteous to the audience to mention them. For instance, Do you feel churchmen show any greater sense of responsibility for supporting good candidates than do nonchurchmen?

The reactant panel could also help the speaker bring out the ways in which many important decisions on issues and candidates are made—before election time ever rolls around and by the handful of persons who really are involved in the work in their political party.

The panel through its questions can help the speaker make clear that, if government is of God (Rom. 13:1-7), all Christians have a responsibility to involve themselves in party activities, for the decisions of political parties are a basic factor in determining whether the authority of the state shall be used to enhance or diminish the God-given quality of freedom for the people.

150

A Demonstration

Joan Kartman and Naomi Hockly were leaving the young-adult church school classroom in animated conversation. As Joan pushed the door open for Naomi, she said, "Up till now I just could not see shoulder safety harnesses."

"Me, too," replied Naomi. "Lap belts were uncomfortable enough until I got used to them."

The pair turned up the sidewalk toward the entrance to the sanctuary. Naomi continued, "But the way he showed us, they may be more comfortable than I thought."

"And," said Joan, "think of the added safety factor. That really impressed me."

They walked up the steps and into the vestibule. As the usher handed them a bulletin, Naomi whispered, "I'm going to check on some tomorrow."

"Let me know what they cost," said her friend as they took their pew.

Earlier in the morning these two young women had been uninformed, thus unconvinced, on the use of shoulder harnesses. Now they were greatly interested. Why the sudden transformation? Because of a demonstration of shoulder harnesses during the class session.

How did this come about in a church school class?

The unit under study was traffic safety and Christian responsibility. The study had moved through a definition of the problem, the "why" of responsibility, and how the class members could be responsible. The issue of safety belts was raised, and several people doubted their effectiveness. "I'll demonstrate to you how valuable they are," said Ray Fry. He arranged for a demonstration by an expert.

Value of demonstration: What makes a demonstration a valuable teaching procedure?

First, of all, the visual impact. Most persons are visually oriented. When a person can see something, his rate of learning increases and his retention is higher than when he is involved only through words. Whether or not the young women referred to at the beginning of this article finally bought safety harnesses for their automobiles I do not know. But this I do know—if you would ask them in a year or two if they remembered the session when Ray Fry brought the auto expert to class, they would say, "Yes, we sure do."

Second, a demonstration is a valuable teaching tool because it is conclusive. That is, the observers see the complete event. They can see it repeated. They can ask specific questions, and the answers can be supplied immediately. For instance, during the shoulder harness demonstration, Joan asked, "Are those shoulder straps really comfortable?"

The demonstrater replied, "Come sit on the seat and try it on for yourself." The answer to Joan's question was conclusive. Had this same question been asked in a verbal discussion three or four persons could have given detailed, reliable—and unreliable—opinions, and Joan still would not have had the answer to her question.

Personal experience: Even seeing was not believing. But when Joan tried the safety harness herself, the personal experience brought conviction, and conviction led to action. Here was proof that real learning had taken place—it resulted in changed behavior.

"When can demonstration be used in the church school

classroom? We study theological ideas. How can I demonstrate them?" asked a young-adult class leader in a seminar. The instructor responded with the following observations.

True, some ideas cannot be visually demonstrated, as, for example, the existence of God. But even here, a carefully planned demonstration of how to use a Bible with a commentary could lead a person into the contents of the Bible where he might experience God. How to deal with hostility, how to visit a sick person, how to read a curriculum book—all are examples of demonstrations that could be used in the course of study in any adult class.

How to provide a demonstration for class consideration is a good question. It should be clear-cut, not forced. It should not be regarded as entertainment, but should be directly related to the contents of the course.

Timing: When to have a classroom demonstration is a question of timing. Had the shoulder harness demonstration been used at the beginning of the unit on traffic safety and Christian responsibility, members might have rebelled on the grounds that a church school class is no place for such things. But after understanding more fully the Christian concept of stewardship of human life, the class saw the validity of becoming accurately informed.

Providing a demonstration too late is as unfortunate as providing it too early. If the safety harness demonstration had had to be delayed a month because the expert was out of town, it should have been dropped altogether, because already the group would have been deep in another unit of study and many persons would be frustrated at having to drop what they were doing and concentrate on something else.

To be successful a classroom demonstration should be well planned and rehearsed in advance, so that it can be performed without a hitch. Incomplete or unsuccessful demonstrations are often worse than no demonstrations at all. Observers get bored and distracted. So plan well.

An Interview

Sometimes it is helpful to examine in depth the involvement of a particular person, his motivations, his actions, his understanding of what he is doing. For this, the interview is a helpful technique. The interview also aids the learning of the one who does the interviewing. Used properly, this is a two-way street.

The purposes for interviews vary according to the needs of those seeking the information. A list of questions to be asked or topical areas to be explored, plus some research on the subject, will help make an interview more rewarding. Questions about *why, how,* and *what* will yield more fruitful answers than questions that can be answered *yes* or *no.* Determine the focal point for the interview and direct attention to it constantly.

Whom to interview: The person to be interviewed should be, or should have been, directly involved in the program or activity being studied. His own personal experience will be his source of information.

If we want to know what has happened in large movements of former times, such as those for woman suffrage or collective bargaining, several types of persons might be interviewed. Some will have been direct participants—suffragettes, union shop organizers, and so on. Others might have been on the opposing side, served on study commissions, or worked in private or governmental agencies created to handle problems that developed. Still others might be more detached, less involved, but still qualified to serve as a source of accurate information. Fitting this description would be professors of government, labor relations, or politics, who lived through the experiences and have studied the situations carefully.

Current events provide many sources of directly involved persons who can be interviewed. However, these persons often are not objective in their evaluation. Their information may be quite accurate or it may be biased, but their involvement may prejudice their evaluation. The interviewer must be aware of such limitations and attempt to obtain a well-rounded set of viewpoints before making judgments or reaching conclusions.

Focus: The interview can focus on a specific aspect in the interviewee's involvement. The frustrations, failures, and successes encountered can provide helpful insights regarding the problems. In talking with a roving street youth worker, it is possible to learn why so many youth find it difficult to relate meaningfully to one another as well as to adults. These workers experience directly most of the frustrations the youth feel, and are in a position to help understand and appreciate the frustrations that produce school dropouts.

Often it is helpful to see a problem through the eyes of someone else. We all tend to filter out unpleasant and undesired information. By interviewing another person we learn to recognize our own limitations in viewing situations and literally to substitute the view of another. The interview can also be used to help someone with limited vision and understanding to experience new views or receive information in a manner that does not threaten him. A group leader alert to such a need can use the interview as a helpful learning experience for this person.

While the interview is of primary value to the interviewer, it may also be of considerable value to other persons. One person can report to another the results of an interview. Care should be taken to credit the source by saying, for example, "When I was talking with the street youth worker in our community, she told me how her girls reacted to their first trip to a downtown department store."

Tape recording: If it is possible or desirable to report to a group, you might consider tape-recording the interview. Of course, such recording should be done only with the permission of the interviewee. By playing the recording to the group, it is possible to increase their degree of involvement and interest and consequently their learning. If time for such a presentation is limited, the tape recording could be edited in advance. However, be sure to indicate clearly that it has been edited. (Listen to radio news announcers as they introduce just a sentence or two from a recorded comment.) Often the heart of an interview is contained in one or two key sentences by the interviewee, and only these are needed for a group to get an accurate understanding of the view being expressed.

Whether interviewing or receiving a report of an interview, we learn much about the subject, the persons involved in it, and our own limitations of knowledge and commitment. If we know the purpose of the interview, the position taken by the interviewee and interviewer regarding the subject, and if we examine the interview carefully, we can learn much about the personal involvement, historical data, significance, and impact of social change in our culture as it is experienced by different people. Then we can evaluate responses and relate our learning to our own needs. The interview can help provide a basis for further study, action, and understanding for individuals and groups.

A Case Study

An effective learning technique is the case study. One learns by direct involvement in a situation. Facts can be obtained which can be used to support or contradict hearsay, rumors, guesses, or other forms of unverified ideas. The actual needs of a situation can be discovered accurately.

Specific tasks can be assigned to individuals. Someone can get data on one phase of a question, while others take responsibility for other types of information. Everyone in a group should have the opportunity to contribute in some way to the total study. Some effort is required to go directly into a situation, to sources such as libraries and private or governmental agencies, in seeking out information for a case study. Learning is more effective because of such personal involvement.

Nature of social change: The case study method is particularly useful in understanding the nature of social change. It is possible to study existing conditions in a particular area, such as a city block. Specific factors to be identified might include percentage of resident and absentee ownership of residence and business property; the age, race, education, health, and employment of household members; and the types of businesses, where customers come from, and how the businessmen relate to the local population.

After obtaining information describing current conditions (or while that is being done by one person or a committee), the case study could turn to earlier reports for data to be used for comparison and correlation. Then it is possible to locate, identify, and relate the various factors that influence social change in that situation.

Causes of change: A further use of the case study method is for seeking knowledge and understanding about the causes of change. Before we respond to the challenge of a situation we need to have answers to such questions as:

Who was the instrument of change? Why was he? What methods were used? With what results? For what reason? Also, it is important to identify whether the change is voluntary or involuntary, provoked or spontaneous, understood by those involved, or misunderstood. In a case study it is possible to pry into the inner workings of a situation with sufficient depth to gain some information for answering these questions.

The case study can center around the local aspect of a larger movement. It might be helpful to examine how the current movement for and against civil rights is affecting the non-English speaking population of a city. Or one might seek to determine whether medicare is really reaching the most needy persons in a town or country. Often it is assumed that a large movement does, or does not, involve us and our neighbors directly. A case study could provide the specific information for forming an accurate picture. Every social movement is rooted in a local expression of some kind. To be responsible Christians we need to understand such relationships before we engage in specific action.

Recommendations: A case study is properly concluded with recommendations for action, further study, long-range planning, or no action. Such recommendations must be clearly related to the facts that study develops. Everyone must understand how the conclusions are reached and why. When the study is made by a group, much of the learning can take place as recommendations are developed through group discussion. Each person has an opportunity to test his ideas, hear those of others, examine his feelings, and determine a resulting viewpoint.

Once a case study has been completed, the decision as to the method of reporting the findings to others must be reached. Now the task is to transfer to others the information and involvement of those who made the study. Those who did not make the study will need, and should have, a learning experience also. The level of awareness of the audience will indicate where to begin. If the report is to be made to an official board that previously asked for the study to be made, the report begins with the findings. But if there has been little awareness of the need for more information, the report must begin by first seeking to create an awareness of the nature of the situation. The creative use of photography and sound, as with slides and tape recordings, can make the learning more effective.

Goals: The learning goals of a case study may include (1) greater and more accurate group information, (2) greater emotional involvement, (3) more relevant action, and (4) more helpful interaction between groups. In studying social change the case study method helps us identify what changes actually take place, how and why the persons involved made the various choices that caused the change, and what further possibilities for change might exist. From such findings it should be possible to determine what should be done next, why, and how.

Learning that leads to concrete action reinforces the previous learning, and it provides greater motivation for more learning in the future. The case study is an effective technique that can be used individually or by any size group willing to become involved.

Planning a Field Trip

Suppose you are preparing to teach "Affluence and Poverty: Dilemma for Christians." Or as a member of a planning committee drawn from a young adult class, you are asking how your class may study affluence and poverty. Should you plan a field trip? (Bergevin, *et al.,* define a field trip as "a carefully planned educational tour in which a group visits an object or place of interest for first-hand observation and study."[1])

Should your class plan such a tour? Yes, if—

1. members of your class are largely insulated from the poor who live in your city;

2. members of your class are, for the most part, from one socioeconomic class with little firsthand experience of poverty;

3. members of your class need to see (and smell) for themselves at close range what poverty is;

4. members of your class have difficulty believing the extent and severity of poverty in American life;

5. members of your class are more inclined to think about the statistics of poverty than about the humanity of the poor;

6. members of your class have seldom seen the houses, the clothes, the food, and the faces of the poor.

As the authors of *Adult Education Procedures* say, the field trip should be used "to provide first-hand observation and study of something [slums, for example] that cannot

[1] *Adult Education Procedures* (New York: The Seabury Press, 1963), p. 74.

161

readily be brought to the learning group." A class studying poverty may fail to study poor people. A field trip can give your class a direct, face-to-face experience of poverty, its surroundings and its victims.

Your class probably needs more than information about the poor. It may also need concern for the poor. A field trip can build concern as well as supply information. A class can read about poverty and discuss it coolly if it has not seen the poor face to face. There is a place in Christian education for "shock treatment." A unit on affluence and poverty, especially, may call for shock treatment; the field trip may provide it.

In order to plan the field trip, you need to decide where you are going and who will be your guide when you get there. For a guide you should choose someone who has the concern for the poor and the firsthand knowledge of poverty that the field trip should provide for your entire class.

How do you find this guide? Ask yourself, What agencies of government (city, county, state, or federal) work with the poor in my city? Or, What agencies of the church work with the poor here? The guide you need for your field trip will probably be found in one of these agencies. (If you have no idea how to locate such agencies, begin looking under "Social Welfare and Welfare Organizations" in the yellow pages of your telephone directory. This listing, or one similar to it, is in all urban directories. Your trip will probably include agencies working with the poor, as well as pockets of poverty within your city.)

With this much background, let's eavesdrop on a conversation among three young adults who are an exemplary planning committee. The three—Marsha, John, and Andy

162

—have just agreed that a field trip will be useful in their class's study of affluence and poverty.

Three members of your class may read this mock conversation to your class as a way of suggesting that the class consider a field trip:

John: O.K. A field trip it will be. Agreed?

Marsha: Yes, but let's be sure we know why we think a field trip is a good idea in this case.

John: Very well. Let's see if we can tick off a few reasons. Marsha, take notes, please.

Andy: Our class needs some concrete experience to undergird our discussions of poverty.

Marsha: A common experience, such as a walking tour of the slums east of the farmers' market, can give our class a point of reference that may keep our discussions from being too concerned about theory and too little concerned about people.

Andy: After a field trip our class may discuss poverty more concretely. Statistics about "the poor" in general are less concrete and less human than the faces of the poor in our own town.

John: By going as a group, we can help one another see and smell and hear things any one of us alone might miss. After we return we can pool our observations and reactions. We can correct, supplement, and reinforce one another. Along the way we will be getting to know one another better.

Marsha: O.K. I'm sold on the value of a field trip. Now, how do we get ready?

Andy: Some things, of course, are so obvious and routine

that we can just mention them now, so long as we remember to assign responsibility for them later. We need to plan for transportation, liability and health insurance for the tour group, and a definite schedule. We need to plan for meals along the tour and for financing. We need to remember that Jane is extremely hard of hearing and that Tom has a severe limp and tires quickly.

John: We need to contact any social service or welfare agencies we intend to visit and make definite plans with them about what we hope to accomplish, when, where, and how.

Marsha: Let's choose our guide by talking to several different agencies about our goals; then let's be sure our guide understands our goal in making this field trip. Let's have a crystal-clear purpose, and let's make this plain to every agency and person we are to visit along the way.

John: Our class will need some advance study if it is going to get the most out of the trip. We should be ready to suggest some study prior to the tour. Perhaps the guide we choose can meet with us for one or two hours before the trip, maybe a week in advance. He may have a set of slides showing what we should look for. He may suggest some reading for us to do before the trip.

Marsha: Our class will need more than advance preparation. Some follow-up would help consolidate what we learn. Shall we ask class members to take notes, make reports, or carry their cameras? Should one member carry a portable tape recorder to get our guide's commentary on tape? Our class might listen to this tape at a subsequent session and so recall more thoroughly what we have learned. We could appoint a committee of three to analyze and discuss the significance of our field trip for *action*. What are we going to *do* as a result of what we *learn?* We must decide how we are going to analyze, interpret, and apply what we learn on this field trip. After all, we are not going to a zoo—we are going to meet people.

John: If our advance preparation is serious and if our follow-through is thorough, then our class will know that this field trip is meant to be not a lark, but a learning experience.

Andy: Finally, I think all of us on the planning committee should read about field trips in *Adult Education Procedures*.

Assessing Group Growth

Whenever two or more individuals come together, there is a dynamic force among them. This force may cause them to remain separate individuals whose only relationship is their common occupation of the ground on which they stand. Or the force may be a kind of magnet that draws people together in unity of purpose and experience. If they are drawn together by this magnetic force, learning will be deeper because each will complement the other.

These dynamic forces that tie us together are creative in nature. Margaret Kuhn, in *You Can't Be Human Alone,* points out that a group of persons is far more than the sum of the individual members.[1] This is because the collectiveness of the group, the product of the dynamic social forces, has limitless growth.

Paul felt this force when he defined the church as the body of Christ. The church has far more power than the total of those parts that make up the body. The dynamic spiritual force binding the parts together gives the body its unlimited possibilities. Were it not for this force each function of the parts would lack importance. "But God has harmonized the whole body by giving importance of function to the parts which lack apparent importance, that the body should work together as a whole with all the members in sympathetic relationship with one another" (I Cor. 12:24-25 Phillips).

This creative relationship does not automatically happen. It may be the result of a long history of association of the members of the group. More likely it is the product of constant, serious evaluation of the growth of the group.

Unfortunately, when evaluation is mentioned, most groups tend to think about a procedure quickly done, after everything is over. Evaluation should be more than a simple series of quick questions to get some surface reactions at the end of an experience; if that is all it amounts to, such a technique is useless, since the group has no opportunity to use the evaluation to improve its working relationships.

If evaluation is to be meaningful, it must work at getting feedback adequate to help the group become aware of its

[1] (National Council of Churches, 1956), p. 1.

own difficulties, to find out why the difficulties are present, and to know how the difficulties may be corrected. Groups must take at least four steps in order to achieve this depth of self-understanding.

Study goals and objectives: Some leading questions that may be used for individual or group consideration are the following: What are the goals of the group? How were these goals arrived at? How are they related to the goals of all the individuals within the group? How are emergent goals handled?

Progress toward meeting goals: The group needs to look carefully at these questions: How did the group arrive at methods of achieving its goals? In what ways do these methods match the skills of the individual members? How effective are these methods?

Individual participation: To know when an individual is participating within the group takes skill on the part of group members. We have often judged a person's participation by how much he talks. More and more, sensitive groups are realizing that the talker may not be participating at all, while the quiet one may be deeply involved.

An assessment of individual roles within the group may produce a depth understanding at this point. Dorothy Hill in *Leading a Group*[2] lists some of the individual roles as follows:

Group-building and maintenance roles: encouraging,

[2] (Nashville: Board of Education of The United Methodist Church, 1966), pp. 43-44.

mediating, gate keeping, standard setting, following, relaxing tension.

Task function or group-task roles: initiating, information seeking, information giving, opinion giving, clarifying, elaborating, coordinating, orienting, testing, summarizing.

Nonfunctional roles, or self-centered behavior: blocking, aggression, seeking recognition, special pleading for pet concerns, withdrawing, dominating.

An observer appointed to watch for these roles could be very helpful to the group members in their attempts to see themselves. Self-understanding is the first step toward good interpersonal relationships.

Determine direction: The simple question, Where do we go from here? may be used to start the group discussing the direction of its consideration. Usually, a new direction is the result of new clarity and assessment of goals.

Sometimes many of the above discussed items can be brought together in a questionnaire like this: [3]

	Yes	No
1. Did you help to formulate the goals for this session?	___	___
2. Was the subject matter interesting to you?	___	___
3. When you arrived today, had you completed the assignments made at the end of the last session?	___	___

[3] From resource packet for *God With Us* (Nashville: Graded Press, 1967).

	Yes	No
4. Did the study book cause you to think about any questions you had never thought about before?	____	____
5. Did the selected readings help you think from more than one point of view?	____	____
6. Did the leaders make it easy for you to participate?	____	____
7. Did you feel that others made a serious effort to understand your point of view?	____	____
8. Does your presence in this group seem more important to you because of this session?	____	____
9. Are you likely to study and think further about the subject matter of this session?	____	____
10. Did any familiar ideas take on unexpected meanings for you?	____	____
11. Do you think the goals of this session were accomplished?	____	____

After the group has tallied its reactions to such a questionnaire, the questions may form the basis for new ways of working.

Biographical Notes

Kenneth Barringer is director of adult work and campus ministry, Division of Christian Education, Iowa Area of The United Methodist Church.

T. Leo Brannon is Director of Methodist Information of the Birmingham Area of The United Methodist Church, Birmingham, Alabama.

Stanley F. Knock, Jr., is minister of education, Union Square Methodist Church, Baltimore, Maryland.

James Leedy is a layman who lives in North Augusta, South Carolina.

L. Paul Neufer is assistant professor of religion and director of religious activities at Lycoming College, Williamsport, Pennsylvania.

Wright Pillow is minister of education at Galloway Methodist Church, Jackson, Mississippi.

Rodney Shaw is projects director, Division of Peace and World Order, General Board of Christian Social Concerns, The United Methodist Church, Washington, D.C.

Lon and Mary Speer live in Nashville, Tennessee; Mr. Speer is editor of *Christian Action.*

Bibliography

GENERAL

Adler, Mortimer J. *How to Read a Book*. New York: Simon and Schuster, 1956.

Bergevin, Paul, *et al. Adult Education Procedures*. New York: Seabury Press, 1963.

Bigge, Morris L. *Learning Theories for Teachers*. New York: Harper & Row, 1964.

Bowman, Locke E. *Straight Talk About Teaching in Today's Church*. Philadelphia: The Westminster Press, 1961.

Brameld, Theodore. *Education as Power*. New York: Holt, Rinehart & Winston, 1965.

Clemmons, Robert S. *Education for Churchmanship*. Nashville: Abingdon Press, 1966.

Foster, Virgil E. *Christian Education Where the Learning Is*. Englewood Cliffs, N.J.: Prentice-Hall, 1968.

Fox, Robert, *et al. Diagnosing Classroom Learning Environments*. Chicago: Science Research Associates, 1966.

Frazier, Alexander (ed.) . *Learning More About Learning*. Washington, D.C.: Association for Supervision and Curriculum

Development, a Department of the National Education Association, 1959.

Jackson, B. F. *Communication—Learning for Churchmen.* Nashville: Abingdon Press, 1968.

Jacobs, Norman E. *Christians Learning for Christian Living.* (Christian Discipleship Series, ed. E. Lee Neal and Herschell H. Richmond.) St. Louis: Christian Board of Publication, 1961.

Kidd, J. R. *How Adults Learn.* New York: Association Press, 1959.

Little, Sara. *Learning Together in the Christian Fellowship.* Richmond: John Knox Press, 1956.

Minor, Harold D. *New Ways for a New Day.* Nashville: Graded Press, 1965.

Morrison, Eleanor Shelton, and Foster, Virgil E. *Creative Teaching in the Church.* Englewood Cliffs, N.J.: Prentice-Hall, 1963.

Vieth, Paul H. *How to Teach in the Church School.* Philadelphia: The Westminster Press, 1935.

USING PERSONAL CREATIVITY

Buchanan, Paul C. *The Leader and Individual Motivation.* New York: Association Press, 1962.

Chesler, Mark, and Fox, Robert. *Role-playing Methods in the Classroom.* Chicago: Science Research Associates, 1966.

Klein, Alan. *Role-Playing in Leadership Training and Group Problem Solving.* New York: Association Press.

Kneller, George F. *The Art and Science of Creativity.* New York: Holt, Rinehart & Winston, 1965.

Levit, Grace, and Jennings, Helen. *How to Use Role Playing.* Adult Education Association of the U.S.A., 1956.

Osborn, Alex F. *Applied Imagination.* Rev. ed. New York: Charles Scribner's Sons, 1963.

Parnes, Sidney J., and Harding, Harold F. (eds.). *A Source Book for Creative Thinking.* New York: Charles Scribner's Sons, 1962.

Weschler, Irving R. *The Leader and Creativity.* New York: Association Press, 1962.

USING PRINTED RESOURCES

Flesch, Rudolf. *How to Write, Speak and Think More Effectively.* New York: The New American Library, 1964.

Fosdick, Harry Emerson. *A Guide to Understanding the Bible.* New York: Harper & Row, 1956.

Hall, Edward T. *The Silent Language.* New York: Doubleday, 1959.

Rood, Wayne R. *The Art of Teaching Christianity.* Nashville: Abingdon Press, 1968.

Scott, Nathan A., Jr. (ed.). *The Climate of Faith in Modern Literature.* New York: Seabury Press, 1964.

———(ed.). *Forms of Extremity in the Modern Novel.* Richmond: John Knox Press, 1965.

———(ed.). *Four Ways of Modern Poetry.* John Knox Press, 1965.

———(ed.). *Man in the Modern Theatre.* John Knox Press, 1965.

Somerville, Rose M. *Family Insights Through the Short Story,* ed. Paul Vahanian. New York: Teachers College Press, Columbia University, 1964.

Stewart, Randall. *American Literature and Christian Doctrine.* Baton Rouge: Louisiana State University Press, 1958.

USING AUDIO AND VISUAL TOOLS

Claassen, Willard. *Learning to Lead.* Scottsdale, Pa.: Herald Press, 1963.

Jones, G. William. *Sunday Night at the Movies.* Richmond: John Knox Press, 1967.

McLuhan, Marshall. *Understanding Media: The Extensions of Man.* New York: McGraw-Hill Book Co., 1964.

Miller, William Robert. *The Christian Encounters the World of Pop Music and Jazz.* St. Louis: Concordia Publishing House, 1965.

Sloan, Robert. *The Tape Recorder.* Austin: Visual Instruction Bureau, University of Texas.

PROCEDURES FOR GROUP INVOLVEMENT

Bergevin, Paul, and Morris, Dwight. *A Manual for Discussion Leaders and Participants.* New York: Seabury Press, 1954.

Blake, Robert R., and Mouton, Jane S. *Group Dynamics: Key to Decision Making.* Houston: Gulf Publishing Co., 1961.

Douglass, Paul. *The Group Workshop Way in the Local Church.* New York: Association Press, 1956.

Hill, Dorothy LaCroix. *Leading a Group.* Nashville: Board of Education of The United Methodist Church, 1966.

Leypoldt, Martha M. *40 Ways to Teach in Groups.* Valley Forge, Pa.: The Judson Press, 1967.

McKinley, John. *Creative Methods for Adult Classes.* St. Louis: The Bethany Press, 1960.